Learning scikit-learn: Machine Learning in Python

Experience the benefits of machine learning techniques by applying them to real-world problems using Python and the open source scikit-learn library

Raúl Garreta

Guillermo Moncecchi

BIRMINGHAM - MUMBAI

Learning scikit-learn: Machine Learning in Python

First published: November 2013

Production Reference: 1181113

Published by Packt Publishing Ltd.
Livery Place
35 Livery Street
Birmingham B3 2PB, UK.

ISBN 978-1-78328-193-0

www.packtpub.com

Cover Image by Faiz Fattohi (faizfattohi@gmail.com)

Credits

Authors
Raúl Garreta

Guillermo Moncecchi

Reviewers
Andreas Hjortgaard Danielsen

Noel Dawe

Gavin Hackeling

Acquisition Editors
Kunal Parikh

Owen Roberts

Commissioning Editor
Deepika Singh

Technical Editors
Shashank Desai

Iram Malik

Copy Editors
Sarang Chari

Janbal Dharmaraj

Aditya Nair

Project Coordinator
Aboli Ambardekar

Proofreader
Katherine Tarr

Indexer
Monica Ajmera Mehta

Graphics
Abhinash Sahu

Production Co-ordinator
Pooja Chiplunkar

Cover Work
Pooja Chiplunkar

About the Authors

Raúl Garreta is a Computer Engineer with much experience in the theory and application of Artificial Intelligence (AI), where he specialized in Machine Learning and Natural Language Processing (NLP).

He has an entrepreneur profile with much interest in the application of science, technology, and innovation to the Internet industry and startups. He has worked in many software companies, handling everything from video games to implantable medical devices.

In 2009, he co-founded Tryolabs with the objective to apply AI to the development of intelligent software products, where he performs as the CTO and Product Manager of the company. Besides the application of Machine Learning and NLP, Tryolabs' expertise lies in the Python programming language and has been catering to many clients in Silicon Valley. Raul has also worked in the development of the Python community in Uruguay, co-organizing local PyDay and PyCon conferences.

He is also an assistant professor at the Computer Science Institute of Universidad de la República in Uruguay since 2007, where he has been working on the courses of Machine Learning, NLP, as well as Automata Theory and Formal Languages. Besides this, he is finishing his Masters degree in Machine Learning and NLP. He is also very interested in the research and application of Robotics, Quantum Computing, and Cognitive Modeling. Not only is he a technology enthusiast and science fiction lover (geek) but also a big fan of arts, such as cinema, photography, and painting.

I would like to thank my girlfriend for putting up with my long working sessions and always supporting me. Thanks to my parents, grandma, and aunt Pinky for their unconditional love and for always supporting my projects. Thanks to my friends and teammates at Tryolabs for always pushing me forward. Thanks Guillermo for joining me in writing this book. Thanks Diego Garat for introducing me to the amazing world of Machine Learning back in 2005.

Also, I would like to have a special mention to the open source Python and scikit-learn community for their dedication and professionalism in developing these beautiful tools.

Guillermo Moncecchi is a Natural Language Processing researcher at the Universidad de la República of Uruguay. He received a PhD in Informatics from the Universidad de la República, Uruguay and a Ph.D in Language Sciences from the Université Paris Ouest, France. He has participated in several international projects on NLP. He has almost 15 years of teaching experience on Automata Theory, Natural Language Processing, and Machine Learning.

He also works as Head Developer at the Montevideo Council and has lead the development of several public services for the council, particularly in the Geographical Information Systems area. He is one of the Montevideo Open Data movement leaders, promoting the publication and exploitation of the city's data.

I would like to thank my wife and kids for putting up with my late night writing sessions, and my family, for being there. You are the best I have.

Thanks to Javier Couto for his invaluable advice. Thanks to Raúl for inviting me to write this book. Thanks to all the people of the Natural Language Group and the Instituto de Computación at the Universidad de la República. I am proud of the great job we do every day building the uruguayan NLP and ML community.

About the Reviewers

Andreas Hjortgaard Danielsen holds a Master's degree in Computer Science from the University of Copenhagen, where he specialized in Machine Learning and Computer Vision. While writing his Master's thesis, he was an intern research student in the Lampert Group at the Institute of Science and Technology (IST), Austria in Vienna. The topic of his thesis was object localization using conditional random fields with special focus on efficient parameter learning. He now works as a software developer in the information services industry where he has used scikit-learn for topic classification of text documents. See more on his website at http://www.hjortgaard.net/.

Noel Dawe is a Ph.D. student in the field of Experimental High Energy Particle Physics at Simon Fraser University, Canada. As a member of the ATLAS collaboration, he has been a part of the search team for the Higgs boson using high energy proton-proton collisions at CERN's Large Hadron Collider (LHC) in Geneva, Switzerland. In his free time, he enjoys contributing to open source scientific software, including scikit-learn. He has developed a significant interest toward Machine learning, to the benefit of his research where he has employed many of the concepts and techniques introduced in this book to improve the identification of tau leptons in the ATLAS detector, and later to extract the small signature of the Higgs boson from the vast amount of LHC collision data. He continues to learn and apply new data analysis techniques, some seen as unconventional in his field, to solve the problems of increasing complexity and growing data sets.

Gavin Hackeling is a Developer and Creative Technologist based in New York City. He is a graduate from New York University in Interactive Telecommunications Program.

www.PacktPub.com

Support files, eBooks, discount offers and more

You might want to visit www.PacktPub.com for support files and downloads related to your book.

Did you know that Packt offers eBook versions of every book published, with PDF and ePub files available? You can upgrade to the eBook version at www.PacktPub.com and as a print book customer, you are entitled to a discount on the eBook copy. Get in touch with us at service@packtpub.com for more details.

At www.PacktPub.com, you can also read a collection of free technical articles, sign up for a range of free newsletters and receive exclusive discounts and offers on Packt books and eBooks.

http://PacktLib.PacktPub.com

Do you need instant solutions to your IT questions? PacktLib is Packt's online digital book library. Here, you can access, read and search across Packt's entire library of books.

Why Subscribe?

- Fully searchable across every book published by Packt
- Copy and paste, print and bookmark content
- On demand and accessible via web browser

Free Access for Packt account holders

If you have an account with Packt at www.PacktPub.com, you can use this to access PacktLib today and view nine entirely free books. Simply use your login credentials for immediate access.

Table of Contents

Preface

Suppose you want to predict whether tomorrow will be a sunny or rainy day. You can develop an algorithm that is based on the current weather and your meteorological knowledge using a rather complicated set of rules to return the desired prediction. Now suppose that you have a record of the day-by-day weather conditions for the last five years, and you find that every time you had two sunny days in a row, the following day also happened to be a sunny one. Your algorithm could generalize this and predict that tomorrow will be a sunny day since the sun reigned today and yesterday. This algorithm is a pretty simple example of learning from experience. This is what **Machine Learning** is all about: algorithms that learn from the available data.

In this book, you will learn several methods for building Machine Learning applications that solve different real-world tasks, from document classification to image recognition.

We will use **Python**, a simple, popular, and widely used programming language, and **scikit-learn**, an open source Machine Learning library.

In each chapter, we will present a different Machine Learning setting and a couple of well-studied methods as well as show step-by-step examples that use Python and scikit-learn to solve concrete tasks. We will also show you tips and tricks to improve algorithm performance, both from the accuracy and computational cost point of views.

What this book covers

Chapter 1, Machine Learning – A Gentle Introduction, presents the main concepts behind Machine Learning while solving a simple classification problem: discriminating flower species based on its characteristics.

Chapter 2, Supervised Learning, introduces four classification methods: Support Vector Machines, Naive Bayes, decision trees, and Random Forests. These methods are used to recognize faces, classify texts, and explain the causes for surviving from the Titanic accident. It also presents Linear Models and revisits Support Vector Machines and Random Forests, using them to predict house prices in Boston.

Chapter 3, Unsupervised Learning, describes methods for dimensionality reduction with Principal Component Analysis to visualize high dimensional data in just two dimensions. It also introduces clustering techniques to group instances of handwritten digits according to a similarity measure using the k-means algorithm.

Chapter 4, Advanced Features, shows how to preprocess the data and select the best features for learning, a task called Feature Selection. It also introduces Model Selection: selecting the best method parameters using the available data and parallel computation.

What you need for this book

For running the book's examples, you will need a running Python environment, including the scikit-learn library and NumPy and SciPy mathematical libraries. The source code will be available in the form of IPython notebooks. For *Chapter 4, Advanced Features*, we will also include the Pandas Python library. *Chapter 1, Machine Learning – A Gentle Introduction*, shows how to install them in your operating system.

Who this book is for

This book is intended for programmers who want to add Machine Learning and data-based methods to their programming skills.

Conventions

In this book, you will find a number of styles of text that distinguish between different kinds of information. Here are some examples of these styles, and an explanation of their meaning.

Code words in text are shown as follows: "The SGDClassifier initialization function allows several parameters."

A block of code is set as follows:

```
>>> from sklearn.linear_model import SGDClassifier
>>> clf = SGDClassifier()
>>> clf.fit(X_train, y_train)
```

Any command-line input or output is written as follows:

```
# sudo apt-get install python-matplotlib
```

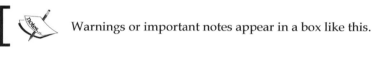 Warnings or important notes appear in a box like this.

 Tips and tricks appear like this.

Reader feedback

Feedback from our readers is always welcome. Let us know what you think about this book—what you liked or may have disliked. Reader feedback is important for us to develop titles that you really get the most out of.

To send us general feedback, simply send an e-mail to feedback@packtpub.com, and mention the book title via the subject of your message.

If there is a topic that you have expertise in and you are interested in either writing or contributing to a book, see our author guide on www.packtpub.com/authors.

Customer support

Now that you are the proud owner of a Packt book, we have a number of things to help you to get the most from your purchase.

Downloading the example code

You can download the example code files for all Packt books you have purchased from your account at http://www.packtpub.com. If you purchased this book elsewhere, you can visit http://www.packtpub.com/support and register to have the files e-mailed directly to you.

Errata

Although we have taken every care to ensure the accuracy of our content, mistakes do happen. If you find a mistake in one of our books—maybe a mistake in the text or the code—we would be grateful if you would report this to us. By doing so, you can save other readers from frustration and help us improve subsequent versions of this book. If you find any errata, please report them by visiting http://www.packtpub.com/submit-errata, selecting your book, clicking on the **errata submission form** link, and entering the details of your errata. Once your errata are verified, your submission will be accepted and the errata will be uploaded on our website, or added to any list of existing errata, under the Errata section of that title. Any existing errata can be viewed by selecting your title from http://www.packtpub.com/support.

Piracy

Piracy of copyright material on the Internet is an ongoing problem across all media. At Packt, we take the protection of our copyright and licenses very seriously. If you come across any illegal copies of our works, in any form, on the Internet, please provide us with the location address or website name immediately so that we can pursue a remedy.

Please contact us at copyright@packtpub.com with a link to the suspected pirated material.

We appreciate your help in protecting our authors, and our ability to bring you valuable content.

Questions

You can contact us at questions@packtpub.com if you are having a problem with any aspect of the book, and we will do our best to address it.

1
Machine Learning – A Gentle Introduction

"I was into data before it was big" – *@ml_hipster*

You have probably heard recently about big data. The Internet, the explosion of electronic devices with tremendous computational power, and the fact that almost every process in our world uses some kind of software, are giving us huge amounts of data every minute.

Think about social networks, where we store information about people, their interests, and their interactions. Think about process-control devices, ranging from web servers to cars and pacemakers, which permanently leave logs of data about their performance. Think about scientific research initiatives, such as the genome project, which have to analyze huge amounts of data about our DNA.

There are many things you can do with this data: examine it, summarize it, and even visualize it in several beautiful ways. However, this book deals with another use for data: as a source of experience to improve our algorithms' performance. These algorithms, which can learn from previous data, conform to the field of Machine Learning, a subfield of Artificial Intelligence.

Any machine learning problem can be represented with the following three concepts:

- We will have to learn to solve a task T. For example, build a spam filter that learns to classify e-mails as spam or ham.

- We will need some experience E to learn to perform the task. Usually, experience is represented through a dataset. For the spam filter, experience comes as a set of e-mails, manually classified by a human as spam or ham.

- We will need a measure of performance P to know how well we are solving the task and also to know whether after doing some modifications, our results are improving or getting worse. The percentage of e-mails that our spam filtering is correctly classifying as spam or ham could be P for our spam-filtering task.

Scikit-learn is an open source Python library of popular machine learning algorithms that will allow us to build these types of systems. The project was started in 2007 as a *Google Summer of Code* project by *David Cournapeau*. Later that year, *Matthieu Brucher* started working on this project as part of his thesis. In 2010, *Fabian Pedregosa*, *Gael Varoquaux*, *Alexandre Gramfort*, and *Vincent Michel* of INRIA took the project leadership and produced the first public release. Nowadays, the project is being developed very actively by an enthusiastic community of contributors. It is built upon NumPy (`http://www.numpy.org/`) and SciPy (`http://scipy.org/`), the standard Python libraries for scientific computation. Through this book, we will use it to show you how the incorporation of previous data as a source of experience could serve to solve several common programming tasks in an efficient and probably more effective way.

In the following sections of this chapter, we will start viewing how to install scikit-learn and prepare your working environment. After that, we will have a brief introduction to machine learning in a practical way, trying to introduce key machine learning concepts while solving a simple practical task.

Installing scikit-learn

Installation instructions for scikit-learn are available at `http://scikit-learn.org/stable/install.html`. Several examples in this book include visualizations, so you should also install the `matplotlib` package from `http://matplotlib.org/`. We also recommend installing IPython Notebook, a very useful tool that includes a web-based console to edit and run code snippets, and render the results. The source code that comes with this book is provided through IPython notebooks.

An easy way to install all packages is to download and install the Anaconda distribution for scientific computing from https://store.continuum.io/, which provides all the necessary packages for Linux, Mac, and Windows platforms. Or, if you prefer, the following sections gives some suggestions on how to install every package on each particular platform.

Linux

Probably the easiest way to install our environment is through the operating system packages. In the case of Debian-based operating systems, such as Ubuntu, you can install the packages by running the following commands:

- Firstly, to install the package we enter the following command:

```
# sudo apt-get install build-essential python-dev python-numpy
python-setuptools python-scipy libatlas-dev
```

- Then, to install matplotlib, run the following command:

```
# sudo apt-get install python-matplotlib
```

- After that, we should be ready to install scikit-learn by issuing this command:

```
# sudo pip install scikit-learn
```

- To install IPython Notebook, run the following command:

```
# sudo apt-get install ipython-notebook
```

- If you want to install from source, let's say to install all the libraries within a virtual environment, you should issue the following commands:

```
# pip install numpy
# pip install scipy
# pip install scikit-learn
```

- To install Matplotlib, you should run the following commands:

```
# pip install libpng-dev libjpeg8-dev libfreetype6-dev
# pip install matplotlib
```

- To install IPython Notebook, you should run the following commands:

```
# pip install ipython
# pip install tornado
# pip install pyzmq
```

Mac

You can similarly use tools such as MacPorts and HomeBrew that contain precompiled versions of these packages.

Windows

To install scikit-learn on Windows, you can download a Windows installer from the downloads section of the project web page: `http://sourceforge.net/projects/scikit-learn/files/`

Checking your installation

To check that everything is ready to run, just open your Python (or probably better, IPython) console and type the following:

```
>>> import sklearn as sk
>>> import numpy as np
>>> import matplotlib.pyplot as plt
```

We have decided to precede Python code with `>>>` to separate it from the sentence results. Python will silently import the scikit-learn, NumPy, and matplotlib packages, which we will use through the rest of this book's examples.

If you want to execute the code presented in this book, you should run IPython Notebook:

```
# ipython notebook
```

This will allow you to open the corresponding notebooks right in your browser.

Datasets

As we have said, machine learning methods rely on previous experience, usually represented by a dataset. Every method implemented on scikit-learn assumes that data comes in a dataset, a certain form of input data representation that makes it easier for the programmer to try different methods on the same data. Scikit-learn includes a few well-known datasets. In this chapter, we will use one of them, the Iris flower dataset, introduced in 1936 by *Sir Ronald Fisher* to show how a statistical method (discriminant analysis) worked (yes, they were into data before it was big). You can find a description of this dataset on its own Wikipedia page, but, essentially, it includes information about 150 elements (or, in machine learning terminology, instances) from three different Iris flower species, including sepal and petal length and width. The natural task to solve using this dataset is to learn to guess the Iris species knowing the sepal and petal measures. It has been widely used on machine learning tasks because it is a very easy dataset in a sense that we will see later. Let's import the dataset and show the values for the first instance:

```
>>> from sklearn import datasets
>>> iris = datasets.load_iris()
>>> X_iris, y_iris = iris.data, iris.target
>>> print X_iris.shape, y_iris.shape
  (150, 4) (150,)
>>> print X_iris[0], y_iris[0]
  [ 5.1  3.5  1.4  0.2] 0
```

Downloading the example code

You can download the example code files for all Packt books you have purchased from your account at http://www.packtpub.com. If you purchased this book elsewhere, you can visit http://www.packtpub.com/support and register to have the files e-mailed directly to you.

We can see that the iris dataset is an object (similar to a dictionary) that has two main components:

- A data array, where, for each instance, we have the real values for sepal length, sepal width, petal length, and petal width, in that order (note that for efficiency reasons, scikit-learn methods work on NumPy ndarrays instead of the more descriptive but much less efficient Python dictionaries or lists). The shape of this array is (150, 4), meaning that we have 150 rows (one for each instance) and four columns (one for each feature).

- A target array, with values in the range of 0 to 2, corresponding to each instance of Iris species (0: setosa, 1: versicolor, and 2: virginica), as you can verify by printing the iris.target.target_names value.

While it's not necessary for every dataset we want to use with scikit-learn to have this exact structure, we will see that every method will require this data array, where each instance is represented as a list of features or attributes, and another target array representing a certain value we want our learning method to learn to predict. In our example, the petal and sepal measures are our real-valued attributes, while the flower species is the one-of-a-list class we want to predict.

Our first machine learning method – linear classification

To get a grip on the problem of machine learning in scikit-learn, we will start with a very simple machine learning problem: we will try to predict the Iris flower species using only two attributes: sepal width and sepal length. This is an instance of a classification problem, where we want to assign a label (a value taken from a discrete set) to an item according to its features.

Let's first build our training dataset—a subset of the original sample, represented by the two attributes we selected and their respective target values. After importing the dataset, we will randomly select about 75 percent of the instances, and reserve the remaining ones (the evaluation dataset) for evaluation purposes (we will see later why we should always do that):

```
>>> from sklearn.cross_validation import train_test_split
>>> from sklearn import preprocessing
>>> # Get dataset with only the first two attributes
>>> X, y = X_iris[:, :2], y_iris
>>> # Split the dataset into a training and a testing set
>>> # Test set will be the 25% taken randomly
>>> X_train, X_test, y_train, y_test = train_test_split(X, y,
  test_size=0.25, random_state=33)
>>> print X_train.shape, y_train.shape
  (112, 2) (112,)
>>> # Standardize the features
>>> scaler = preprocessing.StandardScaler().fit(X_train)
>>> X_train = scaler.transform(X_train)
>>> X_test = scaler.transform(X_test)
```

The `train_test_split` function automatically builds the training and evaluation datasets, randomly selecting the samples. Why not just select the first 112 examples? This is because it could happen that the instance ordering within the sample could matter and that the first instances could be different to the last ones. In fact, if you look at the Iris datasets, the instances are ordered by their target class, and this implies that the proportion of 0 and 1 classes will be higher in the new training set, compared with that of the original dataset. We always want our training data to be a representative sample of the population they represent.

The last three lines of the previous code modify the training set in a process usually called feature scaling. For each feature, calculate the average, subtract the mean value from the feature value, and divide the result by their standard deviation. After scaling, each feature will have a zero average, with a standard deviation of one. This standardization of values (which does not change their distribution, as you could verify by plotting the x values before and after scaling) is a common requirement of machine learning methods, to avoid that features with large values may weight too much on the final results.

Now, let's take a look at how our training instances are distributed in the two-dimensional space generated by the learning feature. `pyplot`, from the matplotlib library, will help us with this:

```
>>> import matplotlib.pyplot as plt
>>> colors = ['red', 'greenyellow', 'blue']
>>> for i in xrange(len(colors)):
>>>     xs = X_train[:, 0][y_train == i]
>>>     ys = X_train[:, 1][y_train == i]
>>>     plt.scatter(xs, ys, c=colors[i])
>>> plt.legend(iris.target_names)
>>> plt.xlabel('Sepal length')
>>> plt.ylabel('Sepal width')
```

The `scatter` function simply plots the first feature value (sepal width) for each instance versus its second feature value (sepal length) and uses the target class values to assign a different color for each class. This way, we can have a pretty good idea of how these attributes contribute to determine the target class. The following screenshot shows the resulting plot:

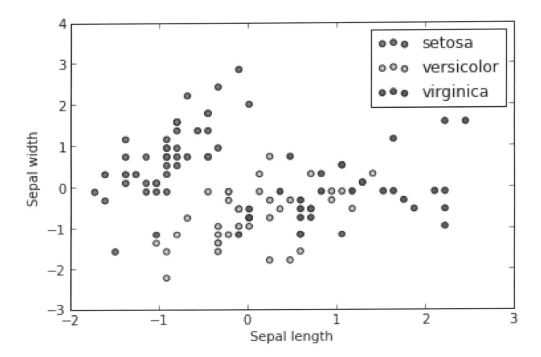

Looking at the preceding screenshot, we can see that the separation between the red dots (corresponding to the Iris setosa) and green and blue dots (corresponding to the two other Iris species) is quite clear, while separating green from blue dots seems a very difficult task, given the two features available. This is a very common scenario: one of the first questions we want to answer in a machine learning task is if the feature set we are using is actually useful for the task we are solving, or if we need to add new attributes or change our method.

Given the available data, let's, for a moment, redefine our learning task: suppose we aim, given an Iris flower instance, to predict if it is a setosa or not. We have converted our problem into a binary classification task (that is, we only have two possible target classes).

If we look at the picture, it seems that we could draw a straight line that correctly separates both the sets (perhaps with the exception of one or two dots, which could lie in the incorrect side of the line). This is exactly what our first classification method, linear classification models, tries to do: build a line (or, more generally, a hyperplane in the feature space) that best separates both the target classes, and use it as a decision boundary (that is, the class membership depends on what side of the hyperplane the instance is).

To implement linear classification, we will use the SGDClassifier from scikit-learn. **SGD** stands for **Stochastic Gradient Descent**, a very popular numerical procedure to find the local minimum of a function (in this case, the loss function, which measures how far every instance is from our boundary). The algorithm will learn the coefficients of the hyperplane by minimizing the loss function.

To use any method in scikit-learn, we must first create the corresponding classifier object, initialize its parameters, and train the model that better fits the training data. You will see while you advance in this book that this procedure will be pretty much the same for what initially seemed very different tasks.

```
>>> from sklearn.linear_modelsklearn._model import SGDClassifier
>>> clf = SGDClassifier()
>>> clf.fit(X_train, y_train)
```

The SGDClassifier initialization function allows several parameters. For the moment, we will use the default values, but keep in mind that these parameters could be very important, especially when you face more real-world tasks, where the number of instances (or even the number of attributes) could be very large. The fit function is probably the most important one in scikit-learn. It receives the training data and the training classes, and builds the classifier. Every supervised learning method in scikit-learn implements this function.

What does the classifier look like in our linear model method? As we have already said, every future classification decision depends just on a hyperplane. That hyperplane is, then, our model. The coef_ attribute of the clf object (consider, for the moment, only the first row of the matrices), now has the coefficients of the linear boundary and the intercept_ attribute, the point of intersection of the line with the y axis. Let's print them:

```
>>> print clf.coef_
[[-28.53692691  15.05517618]
 [ -8.93789454  -8.13185613]
 [ 14.02830747 -12.80739966]]
>>> print clf.intercept_
[-17.62477802  -2.35658325  -9.7570213 ]
```

Indeed in the real plane, with these three values, we can draw a line, represented by the following equation:

-17.62477802 - 28.53692691 * x1 + 15.05517618 * x2 = 0

Now, given *x1* and *x2* (our real-valued features), we just have to compute the value of the left-side of the equation: if its value is greater than zero, then the point is above the decision boundary (the red side), otherwise it will be beneath the line (the green or blue side). Our prediction algorithm will simply check this and predict the corresponding class for any new iris flower.

But, why does our coefficient matrix have three rows? Because we did not tell the method that we have changed our problem definition (how could we have done this?), and it is facing a three-class problem, not a binary decision problem. What, in this case, the classifier does is the same we did — it converts the problem into three binary classification problems in a one-versus-all setting (it proposes three lines that separate a class from the rest).

The following code draws the three decision boundaries and lets us know if they worked as expected:

```
>>> x_min, x_max = X_train[:, 0].min() - .5, X_train[:, 0].max() +
    .5
>>> y_min, y_max = X_train[:, 1].min() - .5, X_train[:, 1].max() +
    .5
>>> xs = np.arange(x_min, x_max, 0.5)
>>> fig, axes = plt.subplots(1, 3)
>>> fig.set_size_inches(10, 6)
>>> for i in [0, 1, 2]:
>>>     axes[i].set_aspect('equal')
>>>     axes[i].set_title('Class '+ str(i) + ' versus the rest')
>>>     axes[i].set_xlabel('Sepal length')
>>>     axes[i].set_ylabel('Sepal width')
>>>     axes[i].set_xlim(x_min, x_max)
>>>     axes[i].set_ylim(y_min, y_max)
>>>     sca(axes[i])
>>>     plt.scatter(X_train[:, 0], X_train[:, 1], c=y_train,
        cmap=plt.cm.prism)
>>>     ys = (-clf.intercept_[i] -
        Xs * clf.coef_[i, 0]) / clf.coef_[i, 1]
>>>     plt.plot(xs, ys, hold=True)
```

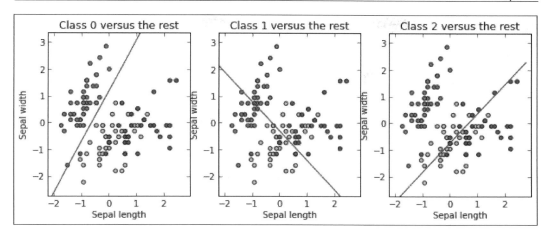

The first plot shows the model built for our original binary problem. It looks like the line separates quite well the Iris setosa from the rest. For the other two tasks, as we expected, there are several points that lie on the wrong side of the hyperplane.

Now, the end of the story: suppose that we have a new flower with a sepal width of 4.7 and a sepal length of 3.1, and we want to predict its class. We just have to apply our brand new classifier to it (after normalizing!). The predict method takes an array of instances (in this case, with just one element) and returns a list of predicted classes:

```
>>>print clf.predict(scaler.transform([[4.7, 3.1]]))
[0]
```

If our classifier is right, this Iris flower is a setosa. Probably, you have noticed that we are predicting a class from the possible three classes but that linear models are essentially binary: something is missing. You are right. Our prediction procedure combines the result of the three binary classifiers and selects the class in which it is more confident. In this case, we will select the boundary line whose distance to the instance is longer. We can check that using the classifier decision_function method:

```
>>>print clf.decision_function(scaler.transform([[4.7, 3.1]]))
[[ 19.73905808    8.13288449 -28.63499119]]
```

Evaluating our results

We want to be a little more formal when we talk about a good classifier. What does that mean? The performance of a classifier is a measure of its effectiveness. The simplest performance measure is accuracy: given a classifier and an evaluation dataset, it measures the proportion of instances correctly classified by the classifier. First, let's test the accuracy on the training set:

```
>>> from sklearn import metrics
>>> y_train_pred = clf.predict(X_train)
>>> print metrics.accuracy_score(y_train, y_train_pred)
0.821428571429
```

This figure tells us that 82 percent of the training set instances are correctly classified by our classifier.

Probably, the most important thing you should learn from this chapter is that measuring accuracy on the training set is really a bad idea. You have built your model using this data, and it is possible that your model adjusts well to them but performs poorly in future (previously unseen data), which is its purpose. This phenomenon is called **overfitting**, and you will see it now and again while you read this book. If you measure based on your training data, you will never detect overfitting. So, never measure based on your training data.

This is why we have reserved part of the original dataset (the testing partition)—we want to evaluate performance on previously unseen data. Let's check the accuracy again, now on the evaluation set (recall that it was already scaled):

```
>>> y_pred = clf.predict(X_test)
>>> print metrics.accuracy_score(y_test, y_pred)
0.684210526316
```

We obtained an accuracy of 68 percent in our testing set. Usually, accuracy on the testing set is lower than the accuracy on the training set, since the model is actually modeling the training set, not the testing set. Our goal will always be to produce models that avoid overfitting when trained over a training set, so they have enough generalization power to also correctly model the unseen data.

Accuracy on the test set is a good performance measure when the number of instances of each class is similar, that is, we have a uniform distribution of classes. But if you have a skewed distribution (say, 99 percent of the instances belong to one class), a classifier that always predicts the majority class could have an excellent performance in terms of accuracy despite the fact that it is an extremely naive method.

Within scikit-learn, there are several evaluation functions; we will show three popular ones: precision, recall, and F1-score (or f-measure). They assume a binary classification problem and two classes—a positive one and a negative one. In our example, the positive class could be Iris setosa, while the other two will be combined into one negative class.

- **Precision**: This computes the proportion of instances predicted as positives that were correctly evaluated (it measures how right our classifier is when it says that an instance is positive).

- **Recall**: This counts the proportion of positive instances that were correctly evaluated (measuring how right our classifier is when faced with a positive instance).

- **F1-score**: This is the harmonic mean of precision and recall, and tries to combine both in a single number.

> The harmonic mean is used instead of the arithmetic mean because the latter compensates low values for precision and with high values for recall (and vice versa). On the other hand, with harmonic mean we will always have low values if either precision or recall is low. For an interesting description of this issue refer to the paper http://www.cs.odu.edu/~mukka/cs795sum12dm/Lecturenotes/Day3/F-measure-YS-26Oct07.pdf

We can define these measures in terms of True and False, and Positives and Negatives:

	Prediction: Positive	**Prediction: Negative**
Target cass: Positive	True Positive (TP)	False Negative (FN)
Target cass: Negative	False Positive (FP)	True Negative (TN)

With m being the sample size (that is, TP + TN + FP + FN), we have the following formulae:

- Accuracy = (TP + TN) / m
- Precision = TP / (TP + FP)
- Recall = TP / (TP + FN)
- F1-score = 2 * Precision * Recall / (Precision + Recall)

Let's see it in practice:

```
>>> print metrics.classification_report(y_test, y_pred,
  target_names=iris.target_names)
              precision   recall  f1-score  support

setosa         1.00       1.00     1.00        8
versicolor     0.43       0.27     0.33       11
virginica      0.65       0.79     0.71       19

avg / total    0.66       0.68     0.66       38
```

We have computed precision, recall, and f1-score for each class and their average values. What we can see in this table is:

- The classifier obtained 1.0 precision and recall in the `setosa` class. This means that for precision, 100 percent of the instances that are classified as setosa are really setosa instances, and for recall, that 100 percent of the setosa instances were classified as setosa.

- On the other hand, in the `versicolor` class, the results are not as good: we have a precision of 0.43, that is, only 43 percent of the instances that are classified as versicolor are really versicolor instances. Also, for versicolor, we have a recall of 0.27, that is, only 27 percent of the versicolor instances are correctly classified.

Now, we can see that our method (as we expected) is very good at predicting `setosa`, while it suffers when it has to separate the `versicolor` or `virginica` classes. The support value shows how many instances of each class we had in the testing set.

Another useful metric (especially for multi-class problems) is the confusion matrix: in its (`i`, `j`) cell, it shows the number of class instances `i` that were predicted to be in class `j`. A good classifier will accumulate the values on the confusion matrix diagonal, where correctly classified instances belong.

```
>>> print metrics.confusion_matrix(y_test, y_pred)
[[ 8  0  0]
 [ 0  3  8]
 [ 0  4 15]]
```

Our classifier is never wrong in our evaluation set when it classifies class `0` (`setosa`) flowers. But, when it faces classes `1` and `2` flowers (`versicolor` and `virginica`), it confuses them. The confusion matrix gives us useful information to know what types of errors the classifier is making.

To finish our evaluation process, we will introduce a very useful method known as cross-validation. As we explained before, we have to partition our dataset into a training set and a testing set. However, partitioning the data, results such that there are fewer instances to train on, and also, depending on the particular partition we make (usually made randomly), we can get either better or worse results. Cross-validation allows us to avoid this particular case, reducing result variance and producing a more realistic score for our models. The usual steps for k-fold cross-validation are the following:

1. Partition the dataset into *k* different subsets.

2. Create *k* different models by training on k-1 subsets and testing on the remaining subset.

3. Measure the performance on each of the *k* models and take the average measure.

Let's do that with our linear classifier. First, we will have to create a composite estimator made by a pipeline of the standardization and linear models. With this technique, we make sure that each iteration will standardize the data and then train/test on the transformed data. The `Pipeline` class is also useful to simplify the construction of more complex models that chain-multiply the transformations. We will chose to have k = 5 folds, so each time we will train on 80 percent of the data and test on the remaining 20 percent. Cross-validation, by default, uses accuracy as its performance measure, but we could select the measurement by passing any scorer function as an argument.

```
>>> from sklearn.cross_validation import cross_val_score, KFold
>>> from sklearn.pipeline import Pipeline
>>> # create a composite estimator made by a pipeline of the
    standarization and the linear model
>>> clf = Pipeline([
        ('scaler', StandardScaler()),
        ('linear_model', SGDClassifier())
])
>>> # create a k-fold cross validation iterator of k=5 folds
>>> cv = KFold(X.shape[0], 5, shuffle=True, random_state=33)
>>> # by default the score used is the one returned by score
    method of the estimator (accuracy)
>>> scores = cross_val_score(clf, X, y, cv=cv)
>>> print scores
[ 0.66666667  0.93333333  0.66666667  0.7         0.6        ]
```

We obtained an array with the *k* scores. We can calculate the mean and the standard error to obtain a final figure:

```
>>> from scipy.stats import sem
>>> def mean_score(scores):
    return ("Mean score: {0:.3f} (+/-
    {1:.3f})").format(np.mean(scores), sem(scores))
>>> print mean_score(scores)
Mean score: 0.713 (+/-0.057)
```

Our model has an average accuracy of 0.71.

Machine learning categories

Classification is only one of the possible machine learning problems that can be addressed with scikit-learn. We can organize them in the following categories:

- In the previous example, we had a set of instances (that is, a set of data collected from a population) represented by certain features and with a particular target attribute. Supervised learning algorithms try to build a model from this data, which lets us predict the target attribute for new instances, knowing only these instance features. When the target class belongs to a discrete set (such as a list of flower species), we are facing a classification problem.

- Sometimes the class we want to predict, instead of belonging to a discrete set, ranges on a continuous set, such as the real number line. In this case, we are trying to solve a **regression** problem (the term was coined by Francis Galton, who observed that the heights of tall ancestors tend to regress down towards a normal value, the average human height). For example, we could try to predict the petal width based on the other three features. We will see that the methods used for regression are quite different from those used for classification.

- Another different type of machine learning problem is that of **unsupervised learning**. In this case, we do not have a target class to predict but instead want to group instances according to some similarity measure based on the available set of features. For example, suppose you have a dataset composed of e-mails and want to group them by their main topic (the task of grouping instances is called **clustering**). We can use it as features, for example, the different words used in each of them.

Important concepts related to machine learning

The linear classifier we presented in the previous section could look too simple. What if we use a higher degree polynomial? What if we also take as features not only the sepal length and width, but also the petal length and the petal width? This is perfectly possible, and depending on the sample distribution, it could lead to a better fit to the training data, resulting in higher accuracy. The problem with this approach is that now we must estimate not only the three original parameters (the coefficients for $x1$, $x2$, and the interception point), but also the parameters for the new features $x3$ and $x4$ (petal length and width) and also the product combinations of the four features.

Intuitively, we would need more training data to adequately estimate these parameters. The number of parameters (and consequently, the amount of training data needed to adequately estimate them) would rapidly grow if we add more features or higher order terms. This phenomenon, present in every machine learning method, is called the idem curse of dimensionality: when the number of parameters of a model grows, the data needed to learn them grows exponentially.

This notion is closely related to the problem of overfitting mentioned earlier. As our training data is not enough, we risk producing a model that could be very good at predicting the target class on the training dataset but fail miserably when faced with new data, that is, our model does not have the generalization power. That is why it is so important to evaluate our methods on previously unseen data.

The general rule is that, in order to avoid overfitting, we should prefer simple (that is, with less parameters) methods, something that could be seen as an instantiation of the philosophical principle of Occam's razor, which states that among competing hypotheses, the hypothesis with the fewest assumptions should be selected.

However, we should also take into account Einstein's words:

> *"Everything should be made as simple as possible, but not simpler."*

The idem curse of dimensionality may suggest that we keep our models simple, but on the other hand, if our model is too simple we run the risk of suffering from underfitting. Underfitting problems arise when our model has such a low representation power that it cannot model the data even if we had all the training data we want. We clearly have underfitting when our algorithm cannot achieve good performance measures even when measuring on the training set.

As a result, we will have to achieve a balance between overfitting and underfitting. This is one of the most important problems that we will have to address when designing our machine learning models.

Other key concepts to take into account are the idem bias and variance of a machine learning method. Consider an extreme method that, in a binary classification setting, always predicts the positive class for any new instance. Its predictions are, trivially, always the same, or in statistical terms, it has null variance; but it will fail to predict negative examples: it is very biased towards positive results. On the other hand, consider a method that predicts, for a new instance, the class of the nearest instance in the training set (in fact, this method exists, and it is called the 1-nearest neighbor). The generalization assumptions that this method uses are very small: it has a very low bias; but, if we change the training data, results could dramatically change, that is, its variance is very high. These are extreme examples of the **bias-variance tradeoff**. It can be shown that, no matter which method we are using, if we reduce bias, variance will increase, and vice versa.

Linear classifiers have generally low-variance: no matter what subset we select for training, results will be similar. However, if the data distribution (as in the case of the versicolor and virginica species) makes target classes not separable by a hyperplane, these results will be consistently wrong, that is, the method is highly biased.

On the other hand, kNN (a memory-based method we will not address in this book) has very low bias but high variance: the results are generally very good at describing training data but tend to vary greatly when trained on different training instances.

There are other important concepts related to real-world applications where our data will not come naturally as a list of real-valued features. In these cases, we will need to have methods to transform non real-valued features to real-valued ones. Besides, there are other steps related to feature standardization and normalization, which as we saw in our Iris example, are needed to avoid undesired effects regarding the different value ranges. These transformations on the feature space are known as **data preprocessing**.

After having a defined feature set, we will see that not all of the features that come in our original dataset could be useful for resolving our task. So we must also have methods to do feature selection, that is, methods to select the most promising features.

In this book, we will present several problems and in each of them we will show different ways to transform and find the most relevant features to use for learning a task, called **feature engineering**, which is based on our knowledge of the domain of the problem and/or data analysis methods. These methods, often not valued enough, are a fundamental step toward obtaining good results.

Summary

In this chapter, we introduced the main general concepts in machine learning and presented scikit-learn, the Python library we will use in the rest of this book. We included a very simple example of classification, trying to show the main steps for learning, and including the most important evaluation measures we will use. In the rest of this book, we plan to show you different machine learning methods and techniques using different real-world examples for each one. In almost every computational task, the presence of historical data could allow us to improve performance in the sense introduced at the beginning of this chapter.

The next chapter introduces supervised learning methods: we have annotated data (that is, instances where the target class/value is known) and we want to predict the same class/value for future data from the same population. In the case of classification tasks, that is, a discrete-valued target class, several different models exist, ranging from statistical methods, such as the simple **Naïve Bayes** to advanced linear classifiers, such as **Support Vector Machines (SVM)**. Some methods, such as **decision trees**, will allow us to visualize how important a feature is to discriminate between different target classes and have a human interpretation of the decision process. We will also address another type of supervised learning task: regression, that is, methods that try to predict real-valued data.

2
Supervised Learning

In *Chapter 1, Machine Learning – A Gentle Introduction*, we sketched the general idea of a supervised learning algorithm. We have the training data where each instance has an input (a set of attributes) and a desired output (a target class). Then we use this data to train a model that will predict the same target class for new unseen instances.

Supervised learning methods are nowadays a standard tool in a wide range of disciplines, from medical diagnosis to natural language processing, image recognition, and searching for new particles at the **Large Hadron Collider (LHC)**. In this chapter we will present several methods applied to several real-world examples by using some of the many algorithms implemented in **scikit-learn**. This chapter does not intend to substitute the scikit-learn reference, but is an introduction to the main supervised learning techniques and shows how they can be used to solve practical problems.

Image recognition with Support Vector Machines

Imagine that the instances in your dataset are points in a multidimensional space; we can assume that the model built by our classifier can be a surface or using linear algebra terminology, a hyperplane that separates instances (points) of one class from the rest. **Support Vector Machines (SVM)** are supervised learning methods that try to obtain these hyperplanes in an optimal way, by selecting the ones that pass through the widest possible gaps between instances of different classes. New instances will be classified as belonging to a certain category based on which side of the surfaces they fall on.

The following figure shows an example for a two-dimensional space with two features (**X1** and **X2**) and two classes (black and white):

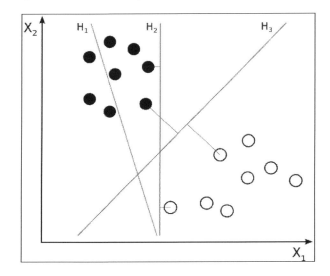

We can observe that the green hyperplane does not separate both classes, committing some classification errors. The blue and the red hyperplanes separate both classes without errors. However, the red surface separates both classes with maximum margin; it is the most distant hyperplane from the closest instances from the two categories. The main advantage of this approach is that it will probably lower the generalization error, making this model resistant to overfitting, something that actually has been verified in several, different, classification tasks.

This approach can be generalized to construct hyperplanes not only in two dimensions, but also in high or infinite dimensional spaces. What is more, we can use nonlinear surfaces, such as polynomial or radial basis functions, by using the so called kernel trick, implicitly mapping inputs into high-dimensional feature spaces.

SVM has become one of the state-of-the-art machine learning models for many tasks with excellent results in many practical applications. One of the greatest advantages of SVM is that they are very effective when working on high-dimensional spaces, that is, on problems which have a lot of features to learn from. They are also very effective when the data is sparse (think about a high-dimensional space with very few instances). Besides, they are very efficient in terms of memory storage, since only a subset of the points in the learning space is used to represent the decision surfaces.

To mention some disadvantages, SVM models could be very calculation intensive while training the model and they do not return a numerical indicator of how confident they are about a prediction. However, we can use some techniques such as K-fold cross-validation to avoid this, at the cost of increasing the computational cost.

We will apply SVM to image recognition, a classic problem with a very large dimensional space (the value of each pixel of the image is considered as a feature). What we will try to do is, given an image of a person's face, predict to which of the possible people from a list does it belongs (this kind of approach is used, for example, in social network applications to automatically tag people within photographs). Our learning set will be a group of labeled images of peoples' faces, and we will try to learn a model that can predict the label of unseen instances. The intuitive and first approach would be to use the image pixels as features for the learning algorithm, so pixel values will be our learning attributes and the individual's label will be our target class.

Our dataset is provided within scikit-learn, so let's start by importing and printing its description.

```
>>> import sklearn as sk
>>> import numpy as np
>>> import matplotlib.pyplot as plt
>>> from sklearn.datasets import fetch_olivetti_faces
>>> faces = fetch_olivetti_faces()
>>> print faces.DESCR
```

The dataset contains 400 images of 40 different persons. The photos were taken with different light conditions and facial expressions (including open/closed eyes, smiling/not smiling, and with glasses/no glasses). For additional information about the dataset refer to http://www.cl.cam.ac.uk/research/dtg/attarchive/facedatabase.html.

Looking at the content of the `faces` object, we get the following properties: `images`, `data`, and `target`. Images contain the 400 images represented as 64 x 64 pixel matrices. `data` contains the same 400 images but as array of 4096 pixels. `target` is, as expected, an array with the target classes, ranging from 0 to 39.

```
>>> print faces.keys()
['images', 'data', 'target', 'DESCR']
>>> print faces.images.shape
(400, 64, 64)
>>> print faces.data.shape
(400, 4096)
>>> print faces.target.shape
(400,)
```

Normalizing the data is important as we saw in the previous chapter. It is also important for the application of SVM to obtain good results. In our particular case, we can verify by running the following snippet that our images already come as values in a very uniform range between 0 and 1 (pixel value):

```
>>> print np.max(faces.data)
1.0
>>> print np.min(faces.data)
0.0
>>> print np.mean(faces.data)
0.547046432495
```

Therefore, we do not have to normalize the data. Before learning, let's plot some faces. We will define the following `helper` function:

```
>>> def print_faces(images, target, top_n):
>>>     # set up the figure size in inches
>>>     fig = plt.figure(figsize=(12, 12))
>>>     fig.subplots_adjust(left=0, right=1, bottom=0, top=1,
        hspace=0.05, wspace=0.05)
>>>     for i in range(top_n):
>>>         # plot the images in a matrix of 20x20
>>>         p = fig.add_subplot(20, 20, i + 1, xticks=[],
        yticks=[])
>>>         p.imshow(images[i], cmap=plt.cm.bone)
>>>
>>>         # label the image with the target value
>>>         p.text(0, 14, str(target[i]))
>>>         p.text(0, 60, str(i))
```

If we print the first 20 images, we can see faces from two persons.

```
>>> print_faces(faces.images, faces.target, 20)
```

Training a Support Vector Machine

To use SVM in scikit-learn to solve our task, we will import the `SVC` class from the `sklearn.svm` module:

```
>>> from sklearn.svm import SVC
```

The **Support Vector Classifier (SVC)** will be used for classification. In the last section of this chapter, we will use SVM for regression tasks.

The SVC implementation has different important parameters; probably the most relevant is `kernel`, which defines the kernel function to be used in our classifier (think of the kernel functions as different similarity measures between instances). By default, the SVC class uses the `rbf` kernel, which allows us to model nonlinear problems. To start, we will use the simplest kernel, the `linear` one.

```
>>> svc_1 = SVC(kernel='linear')
```

Before continuing, we will split our dataset into training and testing datasets.

```
>>> from sklearn.cross_validation import train_test_split
>>> X_train, X_test, y_train, y_test = train_test_split(
    faces.data, faces.target, test_size=0.25, random_state=0)
```

And we will define a function to evaluate K-fold cross-validation.

```
>>> from sklearn.cross_validation import cross_val_score, KFold
>>> from scipy.stats import sem
>>>
>>> def evaluate_cross_validation(clf, X, y, K):
>>>     # create a k-fold croos validation iterator
>>>     cv = KFold(len(y), K, shuffle=True, random_state=0)
>>>     # by default the score used is the one returned by score
    method of the estimator (accuracy)
>>>     scores = cross_val_score(clf, X, y, cv=cv)
>>>     print scores
>>>     print ("Mean score: {0:.3f} (+/-{1:.3f})").format(
        np.mean(scores), sem(scores))

>>> evaluate_cross_validation(svc_1, X_train, y_train, 5)
[ 0.93333333  0.91666667  0.95        0.95        0.91666667]
Mean score: 0.933 (+/-0.007)
```

Cross-validation with five folds, obtains pretty good results (accuracy of 0.933). In a few steps we obtained a face classifier.

We will also define a function to perform training on the training set and evaluate the performance on the testing set.

```
>>> from sklearn import metrics
>>>
>>> def train_and_evaluate(clf, X_train, X_test, y_train, y_test):
>>>
>>>     clf.fit(X_train, y_train)
>>>
>>>     print "Accuracy on training set:"
>>>     print clf.score(X_train, y_train)
>>>     print "Accuracy on testing set:"
>>>     print clf.score(X_test, y_test)
>>>
>>>     y_pred = clf.predict(X_test)
>>>
>>>     print "Classification Report:"
>>>     print metrics.classification_report(y_test, y_pred)
>>>     print "Confusion Matrix:"
>>>     print metrics.confusion_matrix(y_test, y_pred)
```

If we train and evaluate, the classifier performs the operation with almost no errors.

```
>>> train_and_evaluate(svc_1, X_train, X_test, y_train, y_test)
Accuracy on training set:
1.0
Accuracy on testing set:
0.99
```

Let's do a little more, why don't we try to classify the faces as people with and without glasses? Let's do that.

First thing to do is to define the range of the images that show faces wearing glasses. The following list shows the indexes of these images:

```
>>> # the index ranges of images of people with glasses
>>> glasses = [
   (10, 19), (30, 32), (37, 38), (50, 59), (63, 64),
   (69, 69), (120, 121), (124, 129), (130, 139), (160, 161),
   (164, 169), (180, 182), (185, 185), (189, 189), (190, 192),
   (194, 194), (196, 199), (260, 269), (270, 279), (300, 309),
   (330, 339), (358, 359), (360, 369)
]
```

You can check these values by using the `print_faces` function that was defined before to plot the 400 faces and looking at the indexes in the lower-left corners.

Then we'll define a function that from those segments returns a new target array that marks with 1 for the faces with glasses and 0 for the faces without glasses (our new target classes):

```
>>> def create_target(segments):
>>>     # create a new y array of target size initialized with
        zeros
>>>     y = np.zeros(faces.target.shape[0])
>>>     # put 1 in the specified segments
>>>     for (start, end) in segments:
>>>         y[start:end + 1] = 1
>>>     return y
>>> target_glasses = create_target(glasses)
```

So we must perform the training/testing split again.

```
>>> X_train, X_test, y_train, y_test = train_test_split(
        faces.data, target_glasses, test_size=0.25, random_state=0)
```

Now let's create a new SVC classifier, and train it with the new target vector using the following command:

```
>>> svc_2 = SVC(kernel='linear')
```

If we check the performance with cross-validation by the following code:

```
>>> evaluate_cross_validation(svc_2, X_train, y_train, 5)
[ 0.98333333  0.98333333  0.93333333  0.96666667  0.96666667]
Mean score: 0.967 (+/-0.009)
```

We obtain a mean accuracy of 0.967 with cross-validation if we evaluate on our testing set.

```
>>> train_and_evaluate(svc_2, X_train, X_test, y_train, y_test)
Accuracy on training set:
1.0
Accuracy on testing set:
0.99
```

```
Classification Report:
             precision    recall  f1-score   support

          0       1.00      0.99      0.99        67
          1       0.97      1.00      0.99        33

avg / total       0.99      0.99      0.99       100

Confusion Matrix:
[[66  1]
 [ 0 33]]
```

Could it be possible that our classifier has learned to identify peoples' faces associated with glasses and without glasses precisely? How can we be sure that this is not happening and that if we get new unseen faces, it will work as expected? Let's separate all the images of the same person, sometimes wearing glasses and sometimes not. We will also separate all the images of the same person, the ones with indexes from 30 to 39, train by using the remaining instances, and evaluate on our new 10 instances set. With this experiment we will try to discard the fact that it is remembering faces, not glassed-related features.

```
>>> X_test = faces.data[30:40]
>>> y_test = target_glasses[30:40]
>>> print y_test.shape[0]
10
>>> select = np.ones(target_glasses.shape[0])
>>> select[30:40] = 0
>>> X_train = faces.data[select == 1]
>>> y_train = target_glasses[select == 1]
>>> print y_train.shape[0]
390
>>> svc_3 = SVC(kernel='linear')
>>> train_and_evaluate(svc_3, X_train, X_test, y_train, y_test)
Accuracy on training set:
1.0
Accuracy on testing set:
0.9
Classification Report:
             precision    recall  f1-score   support

          0       0.83      1.00      0.91         5
          1       1.00      0.80      0.89         5

avg / total       0.92      0.90      0.90        10
```

```
Confusion Matrix:
[[5 0]
 [1 4]]
```

From the 10 images, only one error, still pretty good results, let's check out which one was incorrectly classified. First, we have to reshape the data from arrays to 64 x 64 matrices:

```
>>> y_pred = svc_3.predict(X_test)
>>> eval_faces = [np.reshape(a, (64, 64)) for a in X_eval]
```

Then plot with our `print_faces` function:

```
>>> print_faces(eval_faces, y_pred, 10)
```

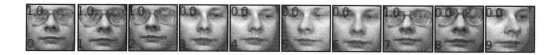

The image number **8** in the preceding figure has glasses and was classified as no glasses. If we look at that instance, we can see that it is different from the rest of the images with glasses (the border of the glasses cannot be seen clearly and the person is shown with closed eyes), which could be the reason it has been misclassified.

With a few lines, we created a face classifier with a linear SVM model. Usually we would not get such good results in the first trial. In these cases, (besides looking at different features) we can start tweaking the hyperparameters of our algorithm. In the particular case of SVM, we can try with different kernel functions; if linear does not give good results, we can try with polynomial or RBF kernels. Also the c and the gamma parameters may affect the results. For a description of the arguments and its values, please refer to the scikit-learn documentation.

Text classification with Naïve Bayes

Naïve Bayes is a simple but powerful classifier based on a probabilistic model derived from the Bayes' theorem. Basically it determines the probability that an instance belongs to a class based on each of the feature value probabilities. The naïve term comes from the fact that it assumes that each feature is independent of the rest, that is, the value of a feature has no relation to the value of another feature.

Despite being very simple, it has been used in many domains with very good results. The independence assumption, although a naïve and strong simplification, is one of the features that make the model useful in practical applications. Training the model is reduced to the calculation of the involved conditional probabilities, which can be estimated by counting frequencies of correlations between feature values and class values.

One of the most successful applications of Naïve Bayes has been within the field of **Natural Language Processing (NLP)**. NLP is a field that has been much related to machine learning, since many of its problems can be formulated as a classification task. Usually, NLP problems have important amounts of tagged data in the form of text documents. This data can be used as a training dataset for machine learning algorithms.

In this section, we will use Naïve Bayes for text classification; we will have a set of text documents with their corresponding categories, and we will train a Naïve Bayes algorithm to learn to predict the categories of new unseen instances. This simple task has many practical applications; probably the most known and widely used one is **spam filtering**. In this section we will try to classify newsgroup messages using a dataset that can be retrieved from within scikit-learn. This dataset consists of around 19,000 newsgroup messages from 20 different topics ranging from politics and religion to sports and science.

As usual, we first start by importing our `pylab` environment:

```
>>> %pylab inline
```

Our dataset can be obtained by importing the `fetch_20newgroups` function from the `sklearn.datasets` module. We have to specify if we want to import a part or all of the set of instances (we will import all of them).

```
>>> from sklearn.datasets import fetch_20newsgroups
>>> news = fetch_20newsgroups(subset='all')
```

If we look at the properties of the dataset, we will find that we have the usual ones: `DESCR`, `data`, `target`, and `target_names`. The difference now is that data holds a list of text contents, instead of a `numpy` matrix:

```
>>> print type(news.data), type(news.target), type(news.target_names)
<type 'list'> <type 'numpy.ndarray'> <type 'list'>
>>> print news.target_names
['alt.atheism', 'comp.graphics', 'comp.os.ms-windows.misc', 'comp.sys.
ibm.pc.hardware', 'comp.sys.mac.hardware', 'comp.windows.x', 'misc.
forsale', 'rec.autos', 'rec.motorcycles', 'rec.sport.baseball', 'rec.
sport.hockey', 'sci.crypt', 'sci.electronics', 'sci.med', 'sci.space',
'soc.religion.christian', 'talk.politics.guns', 'talk.politics.
mideast', 'talk.politics.misc', 'talk.religion.misc']
>>> print len(news.data)
18846
>>> print len(news.target)
18846
```

If you look at, say, the first instance, you will see the content of a newsgroup message, and you can get its corresponding category:

```
>>> print news.data[0]
>>> print news.target[0], news.target_names[news.target[0]]
```

Preprocessing the data

Our machine learning algorithms can work only on numeric data, so our next step will be to convert our text-based dataset to a numeric dataset. Currently we only have one feature, the text content of the message; we need some function that transforms a text into a meaningful set of numeric features. Intuitively one could try to look at which are the words (or more precisely, tokens, including numbers or punctuation signs) that are used in each of the text categories, and try to characterize each category with the frequency distribution of each of those words. The `sklearn.feature_extraction.text` module has some useful utilities to build numeric feature vectors from text documents.

Before starting the transformation, we will have to partition our data into training and testing set. The loaded data is already in a random order, so we only have to split the data into, for example, 75 percent for training and the rest 25 percent for testing:

```
>>> SPLIT_PERC = 0.75
>>> split_size = int(len(news.data)*SPLIT_PERC)
>>> X_train = news.data[:split_size]
>>> X_test = news.data[split_size:]
>>> y_train = news.target[:split_size]
>>> y_test = news.target[split_size:]
```

If you look inside the `sklearn.feature_extraction.text` module, you will find three different classes that can transform text into numeric features: `CountVectorizer`, `HashingVectorizer`, and `TfidfVectorizer`. The difference between them resides in the calculations they perform to obtain the numeric features. `CountVectorizer` basically creates a dictionary of words from the text corpus. Then, each instance is converted to a vector of numeric features where each element will be the count of the number of times a particular word appears in the document.

`HashingVectorizer`, instead of constricting and maintaining the dictionary in memory, implements a hashing function that maps tokens into feature indexes, and then computes the count as in `CountVectorizer`.

`TfidfVectorizer` works like the `CountVectorizer`, but with a more advanced calculation called **Term Frequency Inverse Document Frequency (TF-IDF)**. This is a statistic for measuring the importance of a word in a document or corpus. Intuitively, it looks for words that are more frequent in the current document, compared with their frequency in the whole corpus of documents. You can see this as a way to normalize the results and avoid words that are too frequent, and thus not useful to characterize the instances.

Training a Naïve Bayes classifier

We will create a Naïve Bayes classifier that is composed of a feature vectorizer and the actual Bayes classifier. We will use the `MultinomialNB` class from the `sklearn.naive_bayes` module. In order to compose the classifier with the vectorizer, as we saw in *Chapter 1, Machine Learning – A Gentle Introduction*, scikit-learn has a very useful class called `Pipeline` (available in the `sklearn.pipeline` module) that eases the construction of a compound classifier, which consists of several vectorizers and classifiers.

We will create three different classifiers by combining `MultinomialNB` with the three different text vectorizers just mentioned, and compare which one performs better using the default parameters:

```
>>> from sklearn.naive_bayes import MultinomialNB
>>> from sklearn.pipeline import Pipeline
>>> from sklearn.feature_extraction.text import TfidfVectorizer, >>>
HashingVectorizer, CountVectorizer
>>>
>>> clf_1 = Pipeline([
>>>     ('vect', CountVectorizer()),
>>>     ('clf', MultinomialNB()),
>>> ])
```

```
>>> clf_2 = Pipeline([
>>>     ('vect', HashingVectorizer(non_negative=True)),
>>>     ('clf', MultinomialNB()),
>>> ])
>>> clf_3 = Pipeline([
>>>     ('vect', TfidfVectorizer()),
>>>     ('clf', MultinomialNB()),
>>> ])
```

We will define a function that takes a classifier and performs the K-fold cross-validation over the specified x and y values:

```
>>> from sklearn.cross_validation import cross_val_score, KFold
>>> from scipy.stats import sem
>>>
>>> def evaluate_cross_validation(clf, X, y, K):
>>>     # create a k-fold croos validation iterator of k=5 folds
>>>     cv = KFold(len(y), K, shuffle=True, random_state=0)
>>>     # by default the score used is the one returned by score >>>
method of the estimator (accuracy)
>>>     scores = cross_val_score(clf, X, y, cv=cv)
>>>     print scores
>>>     print ("Mean score: {0:.3f} (+/-{1:.3f})").format(
>>>         np.mean(scores), sem(scores))
```

Then we will perform a five-fold cross-validation by using each one of the classifiers.

```
>>> clfs = [clf_1, clf_2, clf_3]
>>> for clf in clfs:
>>>     evaluate_cross_validation(clf, news.data, news.target, 5)
```

These calculations may take some time; the results are as follows:

```
[ 0.86813478  0.86415495  0.86893075  0.85831786  0.8729443 ]
Mean score: 0.866 (+/-0.002)
[ 0.76359777  0.77182276  0.77765986  0.76147519  0.78222812]
Mean score: 0.771 (+/-0.004)
[ 0.86282834  0.85195012  0.86282834  0.85619528  0.87612732]
Mean score: 0.862 (+/-0.004)
```

As you can see CountVectorizer and TfidfVectorizer had similar performances, and much better than HashingVectorizer.

Let's continue with `TfidfVectorizer`; we could try to improve the results by trying to parse the text documents into tokens with a different regular expression.

```
>>> clf_4 = Pipeline([
>>>     ('vect', TfidfVectorizer(
>>>         token_pattern=ur"\b[a-z0-9_\-\.]+[a-z][a-z0->>> 9_\-
>>>         \.]+\b",
>>>     )),
>>>     ('clf', MultinomialNB()),
>>> ])
```

The default regular expression: `ur"\b\w\w+\b"` considers alphanumeric characters and the underscore. Perhaps also considering the slash and the dot could improve the tokenization, and begin considering tokens as *Wi-Fi* and `site.com`. The new regular expression could be: `ur"\b[a-z0-9_\-\.]+[a-z][a-z0-9_\-\.]+\b"`. If you have queries about how to define regular expressions, please refer to the Python `re` module documentation. Let's try our new classifier:

```
>>> evaluate_cross_validation(clf_4, news.data, news.target, 5)
[ 0.87078801  0.86309366  0.87689042  0.86574688  0.8795756 ]
Mean score: 0.871 (+/-0.003)
```

We have a slight improvement from 0.86 to 0.87.

Another parameter that we can use is `stop_words`: this argument allows us to pass a list of words we do not want to take into account, such as too frequent words, or words we do not a priori expect to provide information about the particular topic.

We will define a function to load the stop words from a text file as follows:

```
>>> def get_stop_words():
>>>     result = set()
>>>     for line in open('stopwords_en.txt', 'r').readlines():
>>>         result.add(line.strip())
>>>     return result
```

And create a new classifier with this new parameter as follows:

```
>>> clf_5 = Pipeline([
>>>     ('vect', TfidfVectorizer(
>>>                 stop_words= get_stop_words(),
>>>                 token_pattern=ur"\b[a-z0-9_\-\.]+[a-z][a-z0->>>
9_\-\.]+\b",
>>>         )),
>>>     ('clf', MultinomialNB()),
>>> ])

>>> evaluate_cross_validation(clf_5, news.data, news.target, 5)
[ 0.88989122  0.8837888   0.89042186  0.88325816  0.89655172]
Mean score: 0.889 (+/-0.002)
```

The preceding code shows another improvement from 0.87 to 0.89.

Let's keep this vectorizer and start looking at the MultinomialNB parameters. This classifier has few parameters to tweak; the most important is the alpha parameter, which is a smoothing parameter. Let's set it to a lower value; instead of setting alpha to 1.0 (the default value), we will set it to 0.01:

```
>>> clf_7 = Pipeline([
>>>     ('vect', TfidfVectorizer(
>>>                 stop_words=stop_words,
>>>                 token_pattern=ur"\b[a-z0-9_\-\.]+[a-z][a-z0->>>
9_\-\.]+\b",
>>>         )),
>>>     ('clf', MultinomialNB(alpha=0.01)),
>>> ])

>>> evaluate_cross_validation(clf_7, news.data, news.target, 5)
[ 0.92305651  0.91377023  0.92066861  0.91907668  0.92281167]
Mean score: 0.920 (+/-0.002)
```

The results had an important boost from 0.89 to 0.92, pretty good. At this point, we could continue doing trials by using different values of alpha or doing new modifications of the vectorizer. In *Chapter 4*, *Advanced Features*, we will show you practical utilities to try many different configurations and keep the best one. But for now, let's look a little more at our Naïve Bayes model.

Evaluating the performance

If we decide that we have made enough improvements in our model, we are ready to evaluate its performance on the testing set.

We will define a helper function that will train the model in the entire training set and evaluate the accuracy in the training and in the testing sets. It will also print a classification report (precision and recall on every class) and the corresponding confusion matrix:

```
>>> from sklearn import metrics
>>>
>>> def train_and_evaluate(clf, X_train, X_test, y_train, y_test):
>>>
>>>     clf.fit(X_train, y_train)
>>>
>>>     print "Accuracy on training set:"
>>>     print clf.score(X_train, y_train)
>>>     print "Accuracy on testing set:"
>>>     print clf.score(X_test, y_test)
>>>     y_pred = clf.predict(X_test)
>>>
>>>     print "Classification Report:"
>>>     print metrics.classification_report(y_test, y_pred)
>>>     print "Confusion Matrix:"
>>>     print metrics.confusion_matrix(y_test, y_pred)
```

We will evaluate our best classifier.

```
>>> train_and_evaluate(clf_7, X_train, X_test, y_train, y_test)
Accuracy on training set:
0.99398613273
Accuracy on testing set:
0.913837011885
```

As we can see, we obtained very good results, and as we would expect, the accuracy in the training set is quite better than in the testing set. We may expect, in new unseen instances, an accuracy of around 0.91.

If we look inside the vectorizer, we can see which tokens have been used to create our dictionary:

```
>>> print len(clf_7.named_steps['vect'].get_feature_names())

61236
```

This shows that the dictionary is composed of 61236 tokens. Let's print the feature names.

```
>>> clf_7.named_steps['vect'].get_feature_names()
```

The following table presents an extract of the results:

Extract of features obtained by vectorizer	
u''sanctuaries'',	u''sanderson'',
u''sanctuary'',	u''sandia'',
u''sanctum'',	u''sandiego.ncr.com'',
u''sand'',	u''sanding'',
u''sandals'',	u''sandlak'',
u''sandbags'',	u''sandman.caltech.edu'',
u''sandberg'',	u''sandman.ece.clarkson.edu'',
u''sandblasting'',	u''sandra'',
u''sanders'',	u''sandro'',
	u''sands''

You can see that some words are semantically very similar, for example, sand and sands, sanctuaries and sanctuary. Perhaps if the plurals and the singulars are counted to the same bucket, we would better represent the documents. This is a very common task, which could be solved using stemming, a technique that relates two words having the same lexical root.

Explaining Titanic hypothesis with decision trees

A common argument against linear classifiers and against statistical learning methods is that it is difficult to explain how the built model decides its predictions for the target classes. If you have a highly dimensional SVM, it is impossible for a human being to even imagine how the hyperplane built looks like. A Naïve Bayes classifier will tell you something like: "this class is the most probable, assuming it comes from a similar distribution as the training data, and making a few more assumptions" something not very useful, for example, we want to know why this or that mail should be considered as spam.

decision trees are very simple yet powerful supervised learning methods, which constructs a decision tree model, which will be used to make predictions. The following figure shows a very simple decision tree to decide if an e-mail should be considered spam:

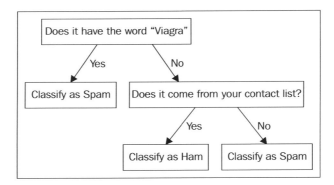

It first asks if the e-mail contains the word **Viagra**; if the answer is yes, it classifies it as spam; if the answer is no, it further asks if it comes from somebody in your contacts list; this time, if the answer is yes, it classifies the e-mail as Ham; if the answer is no, it classify it as spam. The main advantage of this model is that a human being can easily understand and reproduce the sequence of decisions (especially if the number of attributes is small) taken to predict the target class of a new instance. This is very important for tasks such as medical diagnosis or credit approval, where we want to show a reason for the decision, rather than just saying this is what the training data suggests (which is, by definition, what every supervised learning method does). In this section, we will show you through a working example what decision trees look like, how they are built, and how they are used for prediction.

The problem we would like to solve is to determine if a Titanic's passenger would have survived, given her age, passenger class, and sex. We will work with the Titanic dataset that can be downloaded from `http://biostat.mc.vanderbilt.edu/wiki/pub/Main/DataSets/titanic.txt`. Like every other example in this chapter, we start with a dataset that includes the list of Titanic's passengers and a feature indicating whether they survived or not. Each instance in the dataset has the following form:

```
"1","1st",1,"Allen, Miss Elisabeth Walton",29.0000,"Southampton","St
Louis, MO","B-5","24160 L221","2","female"
```

The list of attributes is: Ordinal, Class, Survived (0=no, 1=yes), Name, Age, Port of Embarkation, Home/Destination, Room, Ticket, Boat, and Sex. We will start by loading the dataset into a numpy array.

```
>>> import csv
>>> import numpy as np
>>> with open('data/titanic.csv', 'rb') as csvfile:
>>>     titanic_reader = csv.reader(csvfile, delimiter=',',
>>>     quotechar='"')
>>>
>>>     # Header contains feature names
>>>     row = titanic_reader.next()
>>>     feature_names = np.array(row)
>>>
>>>     # Load dataset, and target classes
>>>     titanic_X, titanic_y = [], []
>>>     for row in titanic_reader:
>>>         titanic_X.append(row)
>>>         titanic_y.append(row[2]) # The target value is
>>>         "survived"
>>>
>>>     titanic_X = np.array(titanic_X)
>>>     titanic_y = np.array(titanic_y)
```

The code shown uses the Python csv module to load the data.

```
>>> print feature_names
['row.names' 'pclass' 'survived' 'name' 'age' 'embarked' 'home.dest'
'room' 'ticket' 'boat' 'sex']

>>> print titanic_X[0], titanic_y[0]
['1' '1st' '1' 'Allen, Miss Elisabeth Walton' '29.0000' 'Southampton'
'St Louis, MO' 'B-5' '24160 L221' '2' 'female'] 1
```

Preprocessing the data

The first step we must take is to select the attributes we will use for learning:

```
>>> # we keep class, age and sex
>>> titanic_X = titanic_X[:, [1, 4, 10]]
>>> feature_names = feature_names[[1, 4, 10]]
```

We have selected feature numbers 1, 4, and 10 that is class, age, and sex, based on the assumption that the remaining attributes have no effect on the passenger's survival. Feature selection is an extremely important step while creating a machine learning solution. If the algorithm does not have good features as input, it will not have good enough material to learn from, results won't be good, no matter even if we have the best machine learning algorithm ever designed.

Sometimes the feature selection will be made manually, based on our knowledge of the problem's domain and the machine learning method we are planning to use. Sometimes feature selection may be done by using automatic tools to evaluate and select the most promising ones. In *Chapter 4*, *Advanced Features*, we will talk a bit about these techniques, but for now, we will manually select our attributes. Very specific attributes (such as Name in our case) could result in overfitting (consider a tree that just asks if the name is X, she survived); attributes where there is a small number of instances with each value, present a similar problem (they might not be useful for generalization). We will use class, age, and sex because a priori, we expect them to have influenced the passenger's survival.

Now, our learning data looks like:

```
>>> print feature_names
['pclass' 'age' 'sex']

>>> print titanic_X[12],titanic_y[12]
['1st' 'NA' 'female'] 1
```

We have shown instance number 12 because it poses a problem to solve; one of its features (the age) is not available. We have **missing values**, a usual problem with datasets. In this case, we decided to substitute missing values with the mean age in the training data. We could have taken a different approach, for example, using the most common value in the training data, or the median value. When we substitute missing values, we have to understand that we are modifying the original problem, so we have to be very careful with what we are doing. This is a general rule in machine learning; when we change data, we should have a clear idea of what we are changing, to avoid skewing the final results.

```
>>> # We have missing values for age
>>> # Assign the mean value
>>> ages = titanic_X[:, 1]
>>> mean_age = np.mean(titanic_X[ages != 'NA',
    1].astype(np.float))
>>> titanic_X[titanic_X[:, 1] == 'NA', 1] = mean_age
```

The implementation of decision trees in scikit-learn expects as input a list of real-valued features, and the decision rules of the model would be of the form:

```
Feature <= value
```

For example, age <= 20.0. Our attributes (except for age) are categorical; that is, they correspond to a value taken from a discrete set such as male and female. So, we have to convert categorical data into real values. Let's start with the sex feature. The preprocessing module of scikit-learn includes a LabelEncoder class, whose fit method allows conversion of a categorical set into a 0..K-1 integer, where K is the number of different classes in the set (in the case of sex, just 0 or 1):

```
>>> # Encode sex
>>> from sklearn.preprocessing import LabelEncoder
>>> enc = LabelEncoder()
>>> label_encoder = enc.fit(titanic_X[:, 2])
>>> print "Categorical classes:", label_encoder.classes_
Categorical classes: ['female' 'male']

>>> integer_classes =
    label_encoder.transform(label_encoder.classes_)
>>> print "Integer classes:", integer_classes
Integer classes: [0 1]

>>> t = label_encoder.transform(titanic_X[:, 2])
>>> titanic_X[:, 2] = t
```

The last two sentences transform the values of the sex attribute into 0-1 values, and modify the training set.

```
print feature_names
['pclass' 'age' 'sex']

print titanic_X[12], titanic_y[12]
['1st' '31.1941810427' '0'] 1
```

We still have a categorical attribute: class. We could use the same approach and convert its three classes into 0, 1, and 2. This transformation implicitly introduces an ordering between classes, something that is not an issue in our problem. However, we will try a more general approach that does not assume an ordering, and it is widely used to convert categorical classes into real-valued attributes. We will introduce an additional encoder and convert the class attributes into three new binary features, each of them indicating if the instance belongs to a feature value (1) or (0). This is called **one hot encoding**, and it is a very common way of managing categorical attributes for real-based methods:

```
>>> from sklearn.preprocessing import OneHotEncoder
>>>
>>> enc = LabelEncoder()
>>> label_encoder = enc.fit(titanic_X[:, 0])
>>> print "Categorical classes:", label_encoder.classes_
Categorical classes: ['1st' '2nd' '3rd']

>>> integer_classes =
    label_encoder.transform(label_encoder.classes_).reshape(3, 1)
>>> print "Integer classes:", integer_classes
Integer classes: [[0] [1] [2]]

>>> enc = OneHotEncoder()
>>> one_hot_encoder = enc.fit(integer_classes)
>>> # First, convert classes to 0-(N-1) integers using
    label_encoder
>>> num_of_rows = titanic_X.shape[0]
>>> t = label_encoder.transform(titanic_X[:,
    0]).reshape(num_of_rows, 1)
>>> # Second, create a sparse matrix with three columns, each one
    indicating if the instance belongs to the class
>>> new_features = one_hot_encoder.transform(t)
>>> # Add the new features to titanix_X
>>> titanic_X = np.concatenate([titanic_X,
    new_features.toarray()], axis = 1)
>>> #Eliminate converted columns
>>> titanic_X = np.delete(titanic_X, [0], 1)
>>> # Update feature names
>>> feature_names = ['age', 'sex', 'first_class', 'second_class',
    'third_class']
>>> # Convert to numerical values
>>> titanic_X = titanic_X.astype(float)
>>> titanic_y = titanic_y.astype(float)
```

The preceding code first converts the classes into integers and then uses the `OneHotEncoder` class to create the three new attributes that are added to the array of features. It finally eliminates from training data the original `class` feature.

```
>>> print feature_names
['age', 'sex', 'first_class', 'second_class', 'third_class']

>>> print titanic_X[0], titanic_y[0]
[29.   0.   1.   0.   0.] 1.0
```

We have now a suitable learning set for scikit-learn to learn a decision tree. Also, standardization is not an issue for decision trees because the relative magnitude of features does not affect the classifier performance.

The preprocessing step is usually underestimated in machine learning methods, but as we can see even in this very simple example, it can take some time to make data look as our methods expect. It is also very important in the overall machine learning process; if we fail in this step (for example, incorrectly encoding attributes, or selecting the wrong features), the following steps will fail, no matter how good the method we use for learning.

Training a decision tree classifier

Now to the interesting part; let's build a decision tree from our training data. As usual, we will first separate training and testing data.

```
>>> from sklearn.cross_validation import train_test_split
>>> X_train, X_test, y_train, y_test = train_test_split(titanic_X, >>>
titanic_y, test_size=0.25, random_state=33)
```

Now, we can create a new `DecisionTreeClassifier` and use the `fit` method of the classifier to do the learning job.

```
>>> from sklearn import tree
>>> clf = tree.DecisionTreeClassifier(criterion='entropy',
    max_depth=3,min_samples_leaf=5)
>>> clf = clf.fit(X_train,y_train)
```

`DecisionTreeClassifier` accepts (as most learning methods) several hyperparameters that control its behavior. In this case, we used the **Information Gain (IG)** criterion for splitting learning data, told the method to build a tree of at most three levels, and to accept a node as a leaf if it includes at least five training instances. To explain this and show how decision trees work, let's visualize the model built. The following code assumes you are using IPython and that your Python distribution includes the `pydot` module. Also, it allows generation of **Graphviz** code from the tree and assumes that Graphviz itself is installed. For more information about Graphviz, please refer to `http://www.graphviz.org/`.

```
>>> import pydot,StringIO
>>> dot_data = StringIO.StringIO()
>>> tree.export_graphviz(clf, out_file=dot_data,
    feature_names=['age','sex','1st_class','2nd_class'
    '3rd_class'])
>>> graph = pydot.graph_from_dot_data(dot_data.getvalue())
>>> graph.write_png('titanic.png')
>>> from IPython.core.display import Image
>>> Image(filename='titanic.png')
```

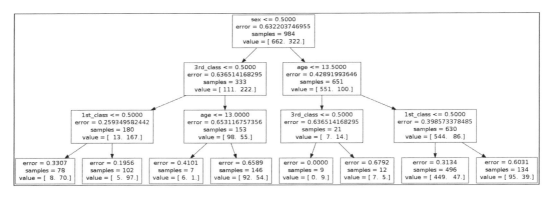

The decision tree we have built represents a series of decisions based on the training data. To classify an instance, we should answer the question at each node. For example, at our root node, the question is: Is sex<=0.5? (are we talking about a woman?). If the answer is yes, you go to the left child node in the tree; otherwise you go to the right child node. You keep answering questions (was she in the third class?, was she in the first class?, and was she below 13 years old?), until you reach a leaf. When you are there, the prediction corresponds to the target class that has most instances (that is if the answers are given to the previous questions). In our case, if she was a woman from second class, the answer would be 1 (that is she survived), and so on.

You might be asking how our method decides which questions should be asked in each step. The answer is **Information Gain** (**IG**) (or the Gini index, which is a similar measure of disorder used by scikit-learn). IG measures how much entropy we lose if we answer the question, or alternatively, how much surer we are after answering it. **Entropy** is a measure of disorder in a set, if we have zero entropy, it means all values are the same (in our case, all instances of the target classes are the same), while it reaches its maximum when there is an equal number of instances of each class (in our case, when half of the instances correspond to survivors and the other half to non survivors). At each node, we have a certain number of instances (starting from the whole dataset), and we measure its entropy. Our method will select the questions that yield more homogeneous partitions (with the lowest entropy), when we consider only those instances for which the answer for the question is yes or no, that is, when the entropy after answering the question decreases.

Interpreting the decision tree

As you can see in the tree, at the beginning of the decision tree growing process, you have the 984 instances in the training set, 662 of them corresponding to class 0 (fatalities), and 322 of them to class 1 (survivors). The measured entropy for this initial group is about 0.632. From the possible list of questions we can ask, the one that produces the greatest information gain is: Was she a woman? (remember that the female category was encoded as 0). If the answer is yes, entropy is almost the same, but if the answer is no, it is greatly reduced (the proportion of men who died was much greater than the general proportion of casualties). In this sense, the woman question seems to be the best to ask. After that, the process continues, working in each node only with the instances that have feature values that correspond to the questions in the path to the node.

If you look at the tree, in each node we have: the question, the initial Shannon entropy, the number of instances we are considering, and their distribution with respect to the target class. In each step, the number of instances gets reduced to those that answer yes (the left branch) and no (the right branch) to the question posed by that node. The process continues until a certain stopping criterion is met (in our case, until we have a fourth-level node, or the number of considered samples is lower than five).

At prediction time, we take an instance and start traversing the tree, answering the questions based on the instance features, until we reach a leaf. At this point, we look at to how many instances of each class we had in the training set, and select the class to which most instances belonged.

For example, consider the question of determining if a 10-year-old girl, from first class would have survived. The answer to the first question (was she female?) is yes, so we take the left branch of the tree. In the two following questions the answers are no (was she from third class?) and yes (was she from first class?), so we take the left and right branch respectively. At this time, we have reached a leaf. In the training set, we had 102 people with these attributes, 97 of them survivors. So, our answer would be survived.

In general, we found reasonable results: the group with more casualties (449 from 496) corresponded to adult men from second or third class, as you can check in the tree. Most girls from first class, on the other side, survived. Let's measure the accuracy of our method in the training set (we will first define a helper function to measure the performance of a classifier):

```
>>> from sklearn import metrics
>>> def measure_performance(X,y,clf, show_accuracy=True,
    show_classification_report=True, show_confussion_matrix=True):
>>>     y_pred=clf.predict(X)
>>>     if show_accuracy:
>>>         print "Accuracy:{0:.3f}".format(
>>>             metrics.accuracy_score(y, y_pred)
>>>         ),"\n"
>>>
>>>     if show_classification_report:
>>>         print "Classification report"
>>>         print metrics.classification_report(y,y_pred),"\n"
>>>
>>>     if show_confussion_matrix:
>>>         print "Confussion matrix"
>>>         print metrics.confusion_matrix(y,y_pred),"\n"

>>> measure_performance(X_train,y_train,clf,
    show_classification=False, show_confusion_matrix=False))
Accuracy:0.838
```

Our tree has an accuracy of 0.838 on the training set. But remember that this is not a good indicator. This is especially true for decision trees as this method is highly susceptible to overfitting. Since we did not separate an evaluation set, we should apply cross-validation. For this example, we will use an extreme case of cross-validation, named **leave-one-out cross-validation**. For each instance in the training sample, we train on the rest of the sample, and evaluate the model built on the only instance left out. After performing as many classifications as training instances, we calculate the accuracy simply as the proportion of times our method correctly predicted the class of the left-out instance, and found it is a little lower (as we expected) than the resubstitution accuracy on the training set.

```
>>> from sklearn.cross_validation import cross_val_score, LeaveOneOut
>>> from scipy.stats import sem
>>>
>>> def loo_cv(X_train, y_train,clf):
>>>     # Perform Leave-One-Out cross validation
>>>     # We are preforming 1313 classifications!
>>>     loo = LeaveOneOut(X_train[:].shape[0])
>>>     scores = np.zeros(X_train[:].shape[0])
>>>     for train_index, test_index in loo:
>>>         X_train_cv, X_test_cv = X_train[train_index],
            X_train[test_index]
>>>         y_train_cv, y_test_cv = y_train[train_index],
            y_train[test_index]
>>>         clf = clf.fit(X_train_cv,y_train_cv)
>>>         y_pred = clf.predict(X_test_cv)
>>>         scores[test_index] = metrics.accuracy_score(
    y_test_cv.astype(int), y_pred.astype(int))
>>>     print ("Mean score: {0:.3f} (+/-{1:.3f})").format(np.
mean(scores), sem(scores))

    >>> loo_cv(X_train, y_train,clf)
Mean score: 0.837 (+/-0.012)
```

The main advantage of leave-one-out cross-validation is that it allows almost as much data for training as we have available, so it is particularly well suited for those cases where data is scarce. Its main problem is that training a different classifier for each instance could be very costly in terms of the computation time.

A big question remains here: how we selected the hyperparameters for our method instantiation? This problem is a general one, it is called model selection, and we will address it in more detail in *Chapter 4, Advanced Features*.

Random Forests – randomizing decisions

A common criticism to decision trees is that once the training set is divided after answering a question, it is not possible to reconsider this decision. For example, if we divide men and women, every subsequent question would be only about men or women, and the method could not consider another type of question (say, age less than a year, irrespective of the gender). **Random Forests** try to introduce some level of randomization in each step, proposing alternative trees and combining them to get the final prediction. These types of algorithms that consider several classifiers answering the same question are called **ensemble methods**. In the Titanic task, it is probably hard to see this problem because we have very few features, but consider the case when the number of features is in the order of thousands.

Random Forests propose to build a decision tree based on a subset of the training instances (selected randomly, with replacement), but using a small random number of features at each set from the feature set. This tree growing process is repeated several times, producing a set of classifiers. At prediction time, each grown tree, given an instance, predicts its target class exactly as decision trees do. The class that most of the trees vote (that is the class most predicted by the trees) is the one suggested by the ensemble classifier.

In scikit-learn, using Random Forests is as simple as importing `RandomForestClassifier` from the `sklearn.ensemble` module, and fitting the training data as follows:

```
>>> from sklearn.ensemble import RandomForestClassifier
>>> clf = RandomForestClassifier(n_estimators=10, random_state=33)
>>> clf = clf.fit(X_train, y_train)
>>> loo_cv(X_train, y_train, clf)
Mean score: 0.817 (+/-0.012)
```

We find that results are actually worse for Random Forests. It seems that introducing randomization was, after all, not a good idea because the number of features was too small. However, for bigger datasets, with a bigger number of features, Random Forests is a very fast, simple, and popular method to improve accuracy, retaining the virtues of decision trees. Actually, in the next section, we will use them for regression.

Evaluating the performance

The final step in every supervised learning task should be to evaluate our best classifier on the previously unseen data, to get an idea of its prediction performance. Remember, this step should not be used to select among competing methods or parameters. That would be cheating (because again, we risk overfitting the new data). So, in our case, let's measure the performance of decision trees on the testing data.

```
>>> clf_dt = tree.DecisionTreeClassifier(criterion='entropy', max_
depth=3, min_samples_leaf=5)
>>> clf_dt.fit(X_train, y_train)
>>> measure_performance(X_test, y_test, clf_dt)
Accuracy:0.793
Classification report
             precision    recall  f1-score   support

          0       0.77      0.96      0.85       202
          1       0.88      0.54      0.67       127

avg / total       0.81      0.79      0.78       329
Confusion matrix
[[193    9]
 [ 59   68]]
```

From the classification results and the confusion matrix, it seems that our method tends to predict too much that the person did not survive.

Predicting house prices with regression

In every example we have seen so far, we have faced what in *Chapter 1, Machine Learning – A Gentle Introduction*, we called classification problems: the output we aimed at predicting belonged to a discrete set. But often, we would want to predict a value extracted from the real line. The learning schema is still the same: fit a model to the training data, and evaluate on new data to get the target class whose value is a real number. Our classifier, instead of selecting a class from a list, should act as a real-valued function, which for each of the (possibly infinite) combination of learning features returns a real number. We could consider regression as classification with an infinite number of target classes.

Many problems can be modeled both as classification and regression tasks, depending on the class we selected as the target. For example, predicting blood sugar level is a regression task, while predicting if somebody has diabetes or not is a classification task.

In the example of the first figure, we have used a line to fit the learning data (composed of a sole attribute and a target value), that is, we have performed linear regression. If we want to predict the value of a new instance, we get their real-valued attribute and obtain the predicted value by projecting the inferred line into the second axis.

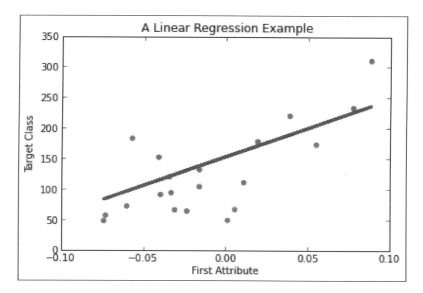

In this section, we will compare several regression methods by using the same dataset. We will try to predict the price of a house as a function of its attributes. As the dataset, we will use the Boston house-prices dataset, which includes 506 instances, representing houses in the suburbs of Boston by 14 features, one of them (the median value of owner-occupied homes) being the target class (for a detailed reference, see `http://archive.ics.uci.edu/ml/datasets/Housing`). Each attribute in this dataset is real-valued.

The dataset is included in the standard scikit-learn distribution, so let's start by loading it:

```
>>> import numpy as np
>>> import matplotlib.pyplot as plt
>>> from sklearn.datasets import load_boston
>>> boston = load_boston()
>>> print boston.data.shape
(506, 13)
>>> print boston.feature_names
['CRIM' 'ZN' 'INDUS' 'CHAS' 'NOX' 'RM' 'AGE' 'DIS' 'RAD' 'TAX'
 'PTRATIO' 'B' 'LSTAT' 'MEDV']
>>> print np.max(boston.target), np.min(boston.target),
    np.mean(boston.target)
50.0 5.0 22.5328063241
```

You should try printing `boston.DESCR` to get a feel of what each feature means. This is a very healthy habit: machine learning is not just number crunching, understanding the problem we are facing is crucial, especially to select the best learning model to use.

As usual, we start slicing our learning set into training and testing datasets, and normalizing the data:

```
>>> from sklearn.cross_validation import train_test_split
>>> X_train, X_test, y_train, y_test =
    train_test_split(boston.data, boston.target, test_size=0.25,
    random_state=33)
>>> from sklearn.preprocessing import StandardScaler
>>> scalerX = StandardScaler().fit(X_train)
>>> scalery = StandardScaler().fit(y_train)
>>> X_train = scalerX.transform(X_train)
>>> y_train = scalery.transform(y_train)
>>> X_test = scalerX.transform(X_test)
>>> y_test = scalery.transform(y_test)
```

Before looking at our best classifier, let's define how we will compare our results. Since we want to preserve our testing set for evaluating the performance of the final classifier, we should find a way to select the best model while avoiding overfitting. We already know the answer: cross-validation. Regression poses an additional problem: how should we evaluate our results? Accuracy is not a good idea, since we are predicting real values, it is almost impossible for us to predict exactly the final value. There are several measures that can be used (you can look at the list of functions under `sklearn.metrics` module). The most common is the **R2** score, or **coefficient of determination** that measures the proportion of the outcomes variation explained by the model, and is the default score function for regression methods in scikit-learn. This score reaches its maximum value of 1 when the model perfectly predicts all the test target values. Using this measure, we will build a function that trains a model and evaluates its performance using five-fold cross-validation and the coefficient of determination.

```
>>> from sklearn.cross_validation import *
>>> def train_and_evaluate(clf, X_train, y_train):
>>>     clf.fit(X_train, y_train)
>>>     print "Coefficient of determination on training
        set:",clf.score(X_train, y_train)
>>>     # create a k-fold cross validation iterator of k=5 folds
>>>     cv = KFold(X_train.shape[0], 5, shuffle=True,
        random_state=33)
>>>     scores = cross_val_score(clf, X_train, y_train, cv=cv)
>>>     print "Average coefficient of determination using 5-fold
        crossvalidation:",np.mean(scores)
```

First try – a linear model

The question that linear models try to answer is which hyperplane in the 14-dimensional space created by our learning features (including the target value) is located closer to them. After this hyperplane is found, prediction reduces to calculate the projection on the hyperplane of the new point, and returning the target value coordinate. Think of our first example in *Chapter 1, Machine Learning – A Gentle Introduction*, where we wanted to find a line separating our training instances. We could have used that line to predict the second learning attribute as a function of the first one, that is, linear regression.

But, what do we mean by closer? The usual measure is least squares: calculate the distance of each instance to the hyperplane, square it (to avoid sign problems), and sum them. The hyperplane whose sum is smaller is the least squares estimator (the hyperplane in the case if two dimensions are just a line).

Since we don't know how our data fits (it is difficult to print a 14-dimension scatter plot!), we will start with a linear model called SGDRegressor, which tries to minimize squared loss.

```
>>> from sklearn import linear_model
>>> clf_sgd = linear_model.SGDRegressor(loss='squared_loss',
    penalty=None, random_state=42)
>>> train_and_evaluate(clf_sgd,X_train,y_train)
Coefficient of determination on training set: 0.743303511411
Average coefficient of determination using 5-fold crossvalidation:
0.715166411086
```

We can print the hyperplane coefficients our method has calculated, which is as follows:

```
>>> print clf_sgd.coef_
[-0.07641527  0.06963738 -0.05935062  0.10878438 -0.06356188
 0.37260998 -0.02912886 -0.20180631  0.08463607 -0.05534634
 -0.19521922 0.0653966 -0.36990842]
```

You probably noted the penalty=None parameter when we called the method. The penalization parameter for linear regression methods is introduced to avoid overfitting. It does this by penalizing those hyperplanes having some of their coefficients too large, seeking hyperplanes where each feature contributes more or less the same to the predicted value. This parameter is generally the L2 norm (the squared sums of the coefficients) or the L1 norm (that is the sum of the absolute value of the coefficients). Let's see how our model works if we introduce an L2 penalty.

```
>>> clf_sgd1 = linear_model.SGDRegressor(loss='squared_loss',
    penalty='l2', random_state=42)
>>> train_and_evaluate(clf_sgd1, X_train, y_train)
Coefficient of determination on training set: 0.743300616394
Average coefficient of determination using 5-fold crossvalidation:
0.715166962417
```

In this case, we did not obtain an improvement.

Second try – Support Vector Machines for regression

The regression version of SVM can be used instead to find the hyperplane.

```
>>> from sklearn import svm
>>> clf_svr = svm.SVR(kernel='linear')
>>> train_and_evaluate(clf_svr, X_train, y_train)
Coefficient of determination on training set: 0.71886923342
Average coefficient of determination using 5-fold crossvalidation:
0.694983285734
```

Here, we had no improvement. However, one of the main advantages of SVM is that (using what we called the kernel trick) we can use a nonlinear function, for example, a polynomial function to approximate our data.

```
>>> clf_svr_poly = svm.SVR(kernel='poly')
>>> train_and_evaluate(clf_svr_poly, X_train, y_train)
Coefficient of determination on training set: 0.904109273301
Average coefficient of determination using 5-fold cross validation:
0.754993478137
```

Now, our results are six points better in terms of coefficient of determination. We can actually improve this by using a **Radial Basis Function (RBF)** kernel.

```
>>> clf_svr_rbf = svm.SVR(kernel='rbf')
>>> train_and_evaluate(clf_svr_rbf, X_train, y_train)
Coefficient of determination on training set: 0.900132065979
Average coefficient of determination using 5-fold cross validation:
0.821626135903
```

RBF kernels have been used in several problems and have shown to be very effective. Actually, RBF is the default kernel used by SVM methods in scikit-learn.

Third try – Random Forests revisited

We can try a very different approach to regression using **Random Forests**. We have previously used Random Forests for classification. When used for regression, the tree growing procedure is exactly the same, but at prediction time, when we arrive at a leaf, instead of reporting the majority class, we return a representative real value, for example, the average of the target values.

Actually, we will use **Extra Trees**, implemented in the `ExtraTreesRegressor` class within the `sklearn.ensemble` module. This method adds an extra level of randomization. It not only selects for each tree a different, random subset of features, but also randomly selects the threshold for each decision.

```
>>> from sklearn import ensemble
>>> clf_et=ensemble.ExtraTreesRegressor(n_estimators=10,
    compute_importances=True, random_state=42)
>>> train_and_evaluate(clf_et, X_train, y_train)
Coefficient of determination on training set: 1.0
Average coefficient of determination using 5-fold cross validation:
0.852511952001
```

The first thing to note is that we have not only completely eliminated underfitting (achieving perfect prediction on training values), but also improved the performance by three points while using cross-validation. An interesting feature of Extra Trees is that they allow computing the importance of each feature for the regression task. Let's compute this importance as follows:

```
>>> print sort(zip(clf_et.feature_importances_,
    boston.feature_names), axis=0)

[['0.000231085384564' 'AGE']
 ['0.000909210196652' 'B']
 ['0.00162702734638' 'CHAS']
 ['0.00292361527201' 'CRIM']
 ['0.00472492264278' 'DIS']
 ['0.00489022243822' 'INDUS']
 ['0.0067481487587' 'LSTAT']
 ['0.00852353178943' 'NOX']
 ['0.00873406149286' 'PTRATIO']
 ['0.0366902590312' 'RAD']
 ['0.0982265323415' 'RM']
 ['0.385904111089' 'TAX']
 ['0.439867272217' 'ZN']]
```

We can see that ZN (proportion of residential land zoned for lots over 25,000 sq. ft.) and TAX (full-value property tax rate) are by far the most influential features on our final decision.

Evaluation

As usual, let's evaluate the performance of our best method on the testing set (previously, we slightly modified our `measure_performance` function to show the coefficient of determination):

```
>>> from sklearn import metrics
>>> def measure_performance(X, y, clf, show_accuracy=True,
        show_classification_report=True, show_confusion_matrix=True,
        show_r2_score=False):
>>>     y_pred = clf.predict(X)
>>>     if show_accuracy:
>>>         print "Accuracy:{0:.3f}".format(
>>>             metrics.accuracy_score(y, y_pred)
>>>         ),"\n"
>>>
>>>     if show_classification_report:
>>>         print "Classification report"
>>>         print metrics.classification_report(y, y_pred),"\n"
>>>
>>>     if show_confusion_matrix:
>>>         print "Confusion matrix"
>>>         print metrics.confusion_matrix(y, y_pred),"\n"
>>>
>>>     if show_r2_score:
>>>         print "Coefficient of determination:{0:.3f}".format(
>>>             metrics.r2_score(y, y_pred)
>>>         ),"\n"

>>> measure_performance(X_test, y_test, clf_et,
        show_accuracy=False, show_classification_report=False,
        show_confusion_matrix=False, show_r2_score=True)
Coefficient of determination:0.793
```

Once we have selected our best method and used all the available data, we could train our best method on the whole training set, but we will have no way to measure its performance on future data, simply because we do not have any more data available.

Summary

In this chapter we reviewed some of the most common supervised learning methods and some practical applications. We learned that supervised methods require instances to have both input features and a target class. In the next chapter, we will review unsupervised learning methods that do not require a target class to be learned. These methods are very useful to understand the structure of the data and can also be used as a previous step before utilizing a supervised learning model.

3
Unsupervised Learning

Nowadays, it is a common assertion that huge amounts of data are available from the Internet for learning. If you read the previous chapters, you will see that even though supervised learning methods are very powerful in predicting future values based on the existing data, they have an obvious drawback: data must be curated; a human being should have annotated the target class for a certain number of instances. This labor is typically done by an expert (if you want to assign the correct species to iris flowers, you need somebody who knows about these flowers at least); it will probably take some time and money to complete, and it will typically not produce significant amounts of data (at least not compared with the Internet!). Every supervised learning building must stand on as much curated data as possible.

However, there are some things we can do without annotated data. Consider the case when you want to assign table seats in a wedding. You want to group people, putting similar people at the same table (the bride's family, the groom's friends, and so on). Anyone that has organized a wedding knows that this task, called **Clustering** in machine learning terminology, is not an easy one. Sometimes people belong to more than one group, and you have to decide if not so similar people can be together (for example, the bride and groom's parents). Clustering involves finding groups where all elements in the group are similar, but objects in different groups are not. What does it mean to be similar is a question every clustering method must answer. The other critical question is how to separate clusters. Humans are very good at finding clusters when faced with two-dimensional data (consider identifying cities in a map just based on the presence of streets), but things become more difficult as dimensions grow.

In this chapter we will present several approximations for clustering: **k-means** (probably the most popular clustering method), **affinity propagation**, **mean shift**, and a model-based method called **Gaussian Mixture Models**.

Another example of unsupervised learning is **Dimensionality Reduction**. Suppose we represent learning instances with a large number of attributes and want to visualize them to identify their principal patterns. This is very difficult when the number of features is more than three, simply because we cannot visualize more than three dimensions. Dimensionality Reduction methods present a way to represent data points of a high dimensional dataset in a lower dimensional space, keeping (at least partly) their pattern structure. These methods are also helpful in selecting the models we should use for learning. For example, if it is reasonable to approximate some supervised learning task using a linear hyperplane or should we resort to more complicated models.

Principal Component Analysis

Principal Component Analysis (PCA) is an orthogonal linear transformation that turns a set of possibly correlated variables into a new set of variables that are as uncorrelated as possible. The new variables lie in a new coordinate system such that the greatest variance is obtained by projecting the data in the first coordinate, the second greatest variance by projecting in the second coordinate, and so on. These new coordinates are called principal components; we have as many principal components as the number of original dimensions, but we keep only those with high variance. Each new principal component that is added to the principal components set must comply with the restriction that it should be orthogonal (that is, uncorrelated) to the remaining principal components. PCA can be seen as a method that reveals the internal structure of data; it supplies the user with a lower dimensional shadow of the original objects. If we keep only the first principal components, data dimensionality is reduced and thus it is easier to visualize the structure of data. If we keep, for example, only the first and second components, we can examine data using a two-dimensional scatter plot. As a result, PCA is useful for exploratory data analysis before building predictive models.

For our learning methods, PCA will allow us to reduce a high-dimensional space into a low-dimensional one while preserving as much variance as possible. It is an unsupervised method since it does not need a target class to perform its transformations; it only relies on the values of the learning attributes. This is very useful for two major purposes:

- **Visualization**: Projecting a high-dimensional space, for example, into two dimensions will allow us to map our instances into a two-dimensional graph. Using these graphical visualizations, we can have insights about the distribution of instances and look at how separable instances from different classes are. In this section we will use PCA to transform and visualize a dataset.

- **Feature selection**: Since PCA can transform instances from high to lower dimensions, we could use this method to address the curse of dimensionality. Instead of learning from the original set of features, we can transform our instances with PCA and then apply a learning algorithm on top of the new feature space.

As a working example, in this section we will use a dataset of handwritten digits digitalized in matrices of 8x8 pixels, so each instance will consist initially of 64 attributes. How can we visualize the distribution of instances? Visualizing 64 dimensions at the same time is impossible for a human being, so we will use PCA to reduce the instances to two dimensions and visualize its distribution in a two-dimensional scatter graph.

We start by loading our dataset (the digits dataset is one of the sample datasets provided with scikit-learn).

```
>>> from sklearn.datasets import load_digits
>>> digits = load_digits()
>>> X_digits, y_digits = digits.data, digits.target
```

If we print the digits keys, we get:

```
>>> print digits.keys()
['images', 'data', 'target_names', 'DESCR', 'target']
```

We will use the `data` matrix that has the instances of 64 attributes each and the `target` vector that has the corresponding digit number.

Let us print the digits to take a look at how the instances will appear:

```
>>> import matplotlib.pyplot as plt
>>> n_row, n_col = 2, 5
>>>
>>> def print_digits(images, y, max_n=10):
>>>     # set up the figure size in inches
>>>     fig = plt.figure(figsize=(2. * n_col, 2.26 * n_row))
>>>     i=0
>>>     while i < max_n and i < images.shape[0]:
>>>         p = fig.add_subplot(n_row, n_col, i + 1, xticks=[],
>>>             yticks=[])
>>>         p.imshow(images[i], cmap=plt.cm.bone,
>>>             interpolation='nearest')
>>>         # label the image with the target value
>>>         p.text(0, -1, str(y[i]))
>>>         i = i + 1
>>>
>>> print_digits(digits.images, digits.target, max_n=10)
```

These instances can be seen in the following diagram:

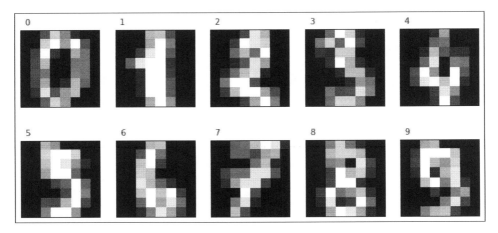

Define a function that will plot a scatter with the two-dimensional points that will be obtained by a PCA transformation. Our data points will also be colored according to their classes. Recall that the target class will not be used to perform the transformation; we want to investigate if the distribution after PCA reveals the distribution of the different classes, and if they are clearly separable. We will use ten different colors for each of the digits, from 0 to 9.

```
>>> def plot_pca_scatter():
>>>     colors = ['black', 'blue', 'purple', 'yellow', 'white',
                'red', 'lime', 'cyan', 'orange', 'gray']
>>>     for i in xrange(len(colors)):
>>>         px = X_pca[:, 0][y_digits == i]
>>>         py = X_pca[:, 1][y_digits == i]
>>>         plt.scatter(px, py, c=colors[i])
>>>     plt.legend(digits.target_names)
>>>     plt.xlabel('First Principal Component')
>>>     plt.ylabel('Second Principal Component')
```

At this point, we are ready to perform the PCA transformation. In scikit-learn, PCA is implemented as a transformer object that learns n number of components through the `fit` method, and can be used on new data to project it onto these components. In scikit-learn, we have various classes that implement different kinds of PCA decompositions, such as `PCA`, `ProbabilisticPCA`, `RandomizedPCA`, and `KernelPCA`. If you need a detailed description of each, please refer to the scikit-learn documentation. In our case, we will work with the `PCA` class from the `sklearn.decomposition` module. The most important parameter we can change is `n_components`, which allows us to specify the number of features that the obtained instances will have. In our case, we want to transform instances of 64 features to instances of just two features, so we will set `n_components` to 2.

Now we perform the transformation and plot the results:

```
>>> from sklearn.decomposition import PCA
>>> estimator = PCA(n_components=10)
>>> X_pca = estimator.fit_transform(X_digits)
>>> plot_pca_scatter()
```

The plotted results can be seen in the following diagram:

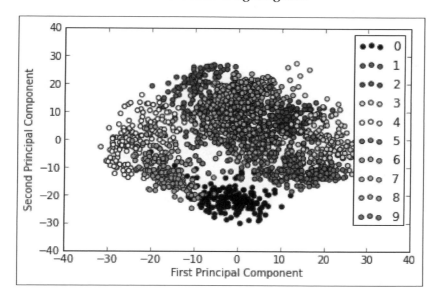

From the preceding figure, we can draw a few interesting conclusions:

- We can view the 10 different classes corresponding to the 10 digits at first sight. We see that for most classes, their instances are clearly grouped in clusters according to their target class, and also that the clusters are relatively distinct. The exception is the class corresponding to the digit **5** with instances very sparsely distributed over the plane overlap with the other classes.

- At the other extreme, the class corresponding to the digit **0** is the most separated cluster. Intuitively, this class may be the one that is easiest to separate from the rest; that is, if we train a classifier, it should be the class with the best evaluation figures.

- Also, for topological distribution, we may predict that contiguous classes correspond to similar digits, which means they will be the most difficult to separate. For example, the clusters corresponding to digits **9** and **3** appear contiguous (which will be expected as their graphical representations are similar), so it might be more difficult to separate a **9** from a **3** than a **9** from a **4**, which is on the left-hand side, far from these clusters.

Notice that we quickly got a graph that gave us a lot of insight into the problem. This technique may be used before training a supervised classifier in order to better understand the difficulties we may encounter. With this knowledge, we may plan better feature preprocessing, feature selection, select a more suitable learning model, and so on. As we mentioned before, it can also be used to perform dimension reduction to avoid the curse of dimensionality and also may allow us to use simpler learning methods, such as linear models.

To finish, let us look at principal component transformations. We will take the principal components from the estimator by accessing the `components` attribute. Each of its components is a matrix that is used to transform a vector from the original space to the transformed space. In the scatter we previously plotted, we only took into account the first two components.

We will plot all the components in the same shape as the original data (digits).

```
>>> def print_pca_components(images, n_col, n_row):
>>>     plt.figure(figsize=(2. * n_col, 2.26 * n_row))
>>>     for i, comp in enumerate(images):
>>>         plt.subplot(n_row, n_col, i + 1)
>>>         plt.imshow(comp.reshape((8, 8)),
>>>             interpolation='nearest')
>>>         plt.text(0, -1, str(i + 1) + '-component')
>>>         plt.xticks(())
>>>         plt.yticks(())
```

The components can be seen as follows:

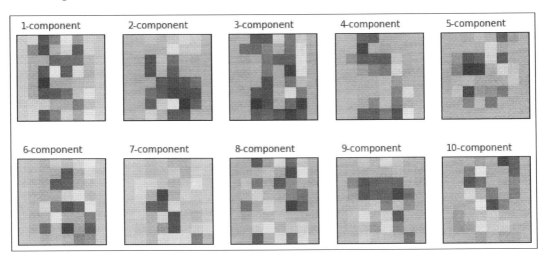

By taking a look at the first two components in the preceding figure, we can draw a few interesting observations:

- If you look at the second component, you can see that it mostly highlights the central region of the image. The `digit` class that is most affected by this pattern is **0**, since its central region is empty. This intuition is confirmed by looking at our previous scatter plot. If you look at the cluster corresponding to the digit **0**, you can see it is the one that has the lower values for the second component.

- Regarding the first component, as we see in the scatter plot, it is very useful to separate the clusters corresponding to the digit **4** (extreme left, low value) and the digit **3** (extreme right, high value). If you see the first component plot, it agrees with this observation. You can see that the regions corresponding to the zone are very similar to the digit **3**, while it has color in the zones that are characteristic of the digit **4**.

If we used additional components, we will get more characteristics to be able to separate the classes into new dimensions. For example, we could add the third principal component and try to plot our instances in a tridimensional scatter plot.

In the next section, we will show another unsupervised group of methods: clustering algorithms. Like dimensionality-reduction algorithms, clustering does not need to know a target class. However, clustering methods try to group instances, looking for those that are (in some way) similar. We will see, however, that clustering methods, like supervised methods, can use PCA to better visualize and analyze their results.

Clustering handwritten digits with k-means

K-means is the most popular clustering algorithm, because it is very simple and easy to implement and it has shown good performance on different tasks. It belongs to the class of partition algorithms that simultaneously partition data points into distinct groups called **clusters**. An alternative group of methods, which we will not cover in this book, are hierarchical clustering algorithms. These find an initial set of clusters and divide or merge them to form new ones.

The main idea behind k-means is to find a partition of data points such that the squared distance between the cluster mean and each point in the cluster is minimized. Note that this method assumes that you know a priori the number of clusters your data should be divided into.

We will show in this section how k-means works using a motivating example, the problem of clustering handwritten digits. So, let us first import our dataset into our Python environment and show how handwritten digits look (we will use a slightly different version of the `print_digits` function we introduced in the previous section).

```
>>> import numpy as np
>>> import matplotlib.pyplot as plt
>>>
>>> from sklearn.datasets import load_digits
>>> from sklearn.preprocessing import scale
>>> digits = load_digits()
>>> data = scale(digits.data)
>>>
>>> def print_digits(images,y,max_n=10):
>>>     # set up the figure size in inches
>>>     fig = plt.figure(figsize=(12, 12))
>>>     fig.subplots_adjust(left=0, right=1, bottom=0, top=1,
>>>        hspace=0.05, wspace=0.05)
>>>     i = 0
>>>     while i <max_n and i <images.shape[0]:
>>>         # plot the images in a matrix of 20x20
>>>         p = fig.add_subplot(20, 20, i + 1, xticks=[],
>>>            yticks=[])
>>>         p.imshow(images[i], cmap=plt.cm.bone)
>>>         # label the image with the target value
>>>         p.text(0, 14, str(y[i]))
>>>         i = i + 1
>>>
>>> print_digits(digits.images, digits.target, max_n=10)
```

The print digits can be seen in the following:

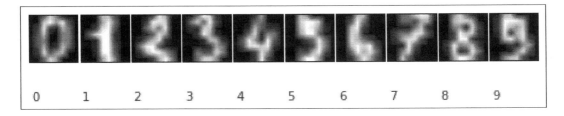

You can see that the dataset contains the corresponding number associated as a target class, but since we are clustering we will not use this information until evaluation time. We will just see if we can group the figures based on their similarity, and form the ten clusters we can expect.

As usual, we must separate train and testing sets as follows:

```
>>> from sklearn.cross_validation import train_test_split
>>> X_train, X_test, y_train, y_test, images_train,
    images_test = train_test_split(
        data, digits.target, digits.images,  test_size=0.25,
            random_state=42)
>>>
>>> n_samples, n_features = X_train.shape
>>> n_digits = len(np.unique(y_train))
>>> labels = y_train
```

Once we have our training set, we are ready to cluster instances. What the k-means algorithm does is:

1. Select an initial set of cluster centers at random.

2. Find the nearest cluster center for each data point, and assign the data point closest to that cluster.

3. Compute the new cluster centers, averaging the values of the cluster data points, and repeat until cluster membership stabilizes; that is, until a few data points change their clusters after each iteration.

Because of how k-means works, it can converge to local minima, and the initial set of cluster centers could greatly affect the clusters found. The usual approach to mitigate this is to try several initial sets and select the set with minimal value for the sum of squared distances between cluster centers (or inertia). The implementation of k-means in scikit-learn already does this (the n-init parameter allows us to establish how many different centroid configurations the algorithm will try). It also allows us to specify that the initial centroids will be sufficiently separated, leading to better results. Let's see how this works on our dataset.

```
>>> from sklearn import cluster
>>> clf = Cluster.KMeans(init='kmeans++',
    n_clusters=10, random_state=42)
>>> clf.fit(X_train)
```

The procedure is similar to the one used for supervised learning, but note that the fit method only takes the training data as an argument. Also observe that we need to specify the number of clusters. We can perceive this number because we know that clusters represent numbers.

If we print the value of the labels_ attribute of the classifier, we get a list of the cluster numbers associated to each training instance.

```
>>> print_digits(images_train, clf.labels_, max_n=10)
```

The cluster can be seen in the following diagram:

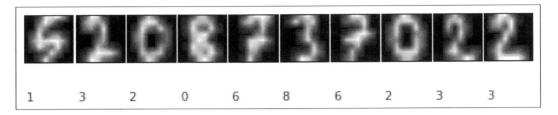

Note that the cluster number has nothing to do with the real number value. Remember that we have not used the class to classify; we only grouped images by similarity. Let's see how our algorithm behaves on the testing data.

To predict the clusters for training data, we use the usual `predict` method of the classifier.

```
>>> y_pred=clf.predict(X_test)
```

Let us see how clusters look:

```
>>> def print_cluster(images, y_pred, cluster_number):
>>>       images = images[y_pred==cluster_number]
>>>       y_pred = y_pred[y_pred==cluster_number]
>>>       print_digits(images, y_pred,max_n=10)
>>> for i in range(10):
>>>       print_cluster(images_test, y_pred, i)
```

This code shows ten images from each cluster. Some clusters are very clear, as shown in the following figure:

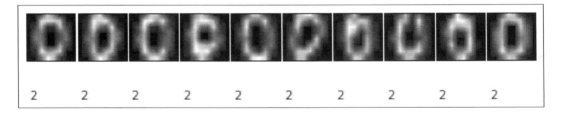

Cluster number **2** corresponds to zeros. What about cluster number **7**?

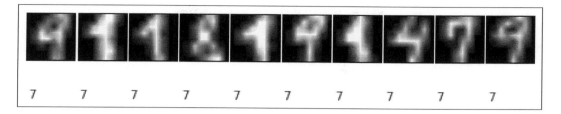

It is not so clear. It seems cluster **7** is something like drawn numbers that look similar to the digit nine. Cluster number **9** only has six instances, as shown in the following figure:

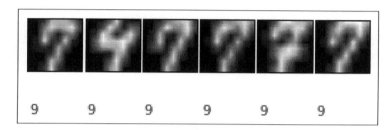

It must be clear after reading that we are not classifying images here (as in the face examples in the previous chapter). We are grouping into ten classes (you can try changing the number of clusters and see what happens).

How can we evaluate our performance? Precision and all that stuff does not work, since we have no target classes to compare with. To evaluate, we need to know the "real" clusters, whatever that means. We can suppose, for our example, that each cluster includes every drawing of a certain number, and only that number. Knowing this, we can compute the **adjusted Rand index** between our cluster assignment and the expected one. The Rand index is a similar measure for accuracy, but it takes into account the fact that classes can have different names in both assignments. That is, if we change class names, the index does not change. The adjusted index tries to deduct from the result coincidences that have occurred by chance. When you have the exact same clusters in both sets, the Rand index equals one, while it equals zero when there are no clusters sharing a data point.

```
>>> from sklearn import metrics
>>> print "Adjusted rand score:
    {:.2}".format(metrics.adjusted_rand_score(y_test, y_pred))
Adjusted rand score:0.57
```

We can also print the confusion matrix as follows:

```
>>> print metrics.confusion_matrix(y_test, y_pred)
[[ 0  0 43  0  0  0  0  0  0  0]
 [20  0  0  7  0  0  0 10  0  0]
 [ 5  0  0 31  0  0  0  1  1  0]
 [ 1  0  0  1  0  1  4  0 39  0]
 [ 1 50  0  0  0  0  1  2  0  1]
 [ 1  0  0  0  1 41  0  0 16  0]
 [ 0  0  1  0 44  0  0  0  0  0]
 [ 0  0  0  0  0  1 34  1  0  5]
 [21  0  0  0  0  3  1  2 11  0]
 [ 0  0  0  0  0  2  3  3 40  0]]
```

Observe that the class 0 in the test set (which coincides with number 0 drawings) is completely assigned to the cluster number 2. We have problems with number 8: 21 instances are assigned class 0, while 11 are assigned class 8, and so on. Not so good after all.

If we want to graphically show how k-means clusters look like, we must plot them on a two-dimensional plane. We have learned how to do that in the previous section: Principal Component Analysis (PCA). Let's construct a **meshgrid** of points (after dimensionality reduction), calculate their assigned cluster, and plot them.

 This example is taken from the very nice scikit-learn tutorial at http://scikit-learn.org/.

```
>>> from sklearn import decomposition
>>> pca = decomposition.PCA(n_components=2).fit(X_train)
>>> reduced_X_train = pca.transform(X_train)
>>> # Step size of the mesh.
>>> h = .01
>>> # point in the mesh [x_min, m_max]x[y_min, y_max].
>>> x_min, x_max = reduced_X_train[:, 0].min() + 1,
    reduced_X_train[:, 0].max() - 1
>>> y_min, y_max = reduced_X_train[:, 1].min() + 1,
    reduced_X_train[:, 1].max() - 1
>>> xx, yy = np.meshgrid(np.arange(x_min, x_max, h),
    np.arange(y_min, y_max, h))
>>> kmeans = cluster.KMeans(init='k-means++', n_clusters=n_digits,
    n_init=10)
```

```
>>> kmeans.fit(reduced_X_train)
>>> Z = kmeans.predict(np.c_[xx.ravel(), yy.ravel()])
>>> # Put the result into a color plot
>>> Z = Z.reshape(xx.shape)
>>> plt.figure(1)
>>> plt.clf()
>>> plt.imshow(Z, interpolation='nearest',
        extent=(xx.min(), xx.max(), yy.min(),
        yy.max()), cmap=plt.cm.Paired, aspect='auto', origin='lower')
>>> plt.plot(reduced_X_train[:, 0], reduced_X_train[:, 1], 'k.',
        markersize=2)
>>> # Plot the centroids as a white X
>>> centroids = kmeans.cluster_centers_
>>> plt.scatter(centroids[:, 0], centroids[:, 1],marker='.',
        s=169, linewidths=3, color='w', zorder=10)
>>> plt.title('K-means clustering on the digits dataset (PCA
        reduced data)\nCentroids are marked with white dots')
>>> plt.xlim(x_min, x_max)
>>> plt.ylim(y_min, y_max)
>>> plt.xticks(())
>>> plt.yticks(())
>>> plt.show()
```

The k-means clustering on the digits dataset can be seen in the following diagram:

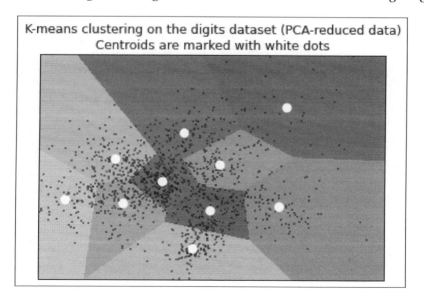

Alternative clustering methods

The scikit-learn toolkit includes several clustering algorithms, all of them including similar methods and parameters to those we used in k-means. In this section we will briefly review some of them, suggesting some of their advantages.

A typical problem for clustering is that most methods require the number of clusters we want to identify. The general approach to solve this is to try different numbers and let an expert determine which works best using techniques such as dimensionality reduction to visualize clusters. There are also some methods that try to automatically calculate the number of clusters. Scikit-learn includes an implementation of **Affinity Propagation**, a method that looks for instances that are the most representative of others, and uses them to describe the clusters. Let's see how it works on our digit-learning problem:

```
>>> aff = cluster.AffinityPropagation()
>>> aff.fit(X_train)
>>> print aff.cluster_centers_indices_.shape
(112,)
```

Affinity propagation detected 112 clusters in our training set. It seems, after all, that the numbers are not so similar between them. You can try drawing the clusters using the print_digits function, and see which clusters seemed to group. The cluster_ centers_indices_ attribute represents what Affinity Propagation found as the canonical elements of each cluster.

Another method that calculates cluster number is MeanShift(). If we apply it to our example, it detects 18 clusters as follows:

```
>>> ms = cluster.MeanShift()
>>> ms.fit(X_train)
>>> print ms.cluster_centers_.shape
(18, 64)
```

In this case, the cluster_centers_ attribute shows the hyperplane cluster centroids. The two previous examples show that results can vary a lot depending on the method we are using. Which clustering method to use depends on the problem we are solving and the type of clusters we want to find.

Note that, for the last two methods, we cannot use the Rand score to evaluate performance because we do not have a canonical set of clusters to compare with. We can, however, measure the inertia of the clustering, since inertia is the sum of distances from each data point to the centroid; we expect near-zero numbers. Unfortunately, there is currently no way in scikit-learn to measure inertia except for the k-means method.

Finally, we will try a probabilistic approach to clustering, using **Gaussian Mixture Models (GMM)**. We will see, from a procedural view, that it is very similar to k-means, but their theoretical principles are quite different. GMM assumes that data comes from a mixture of finite Gaussian distributions with unknown parameters. A Gaussian distribution is a well-known distribution function within statistics used to model many phenomena. It has a bell shaped function centered in the mean value; you have probably seen the following drawing before:

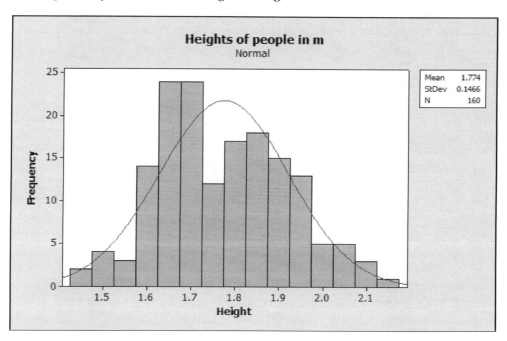

If we take a sufficiently large sample of men and measure their height, the histogram (proportion of men with each specific height) can be adjusted by a Gaussian distribution with mean 1.774 meters and standard deviation of 0.1466 meters. Mean indicates the most probable value (which coincides with the peak of the curve), and standard deviation indicates how spread out the results are; that is, how far they can appear from the mean values. If we measure the area beneath the curve (that is, its integral) between two specific heights, we can know, given a man, how probable it is that his height lies between the two values, in case the distribution is correct. Now, why should we expect that distribution and not another? Actually, not every phenomenon has the same distribution, but a theorem called the **Law of Large Numbers** tells us that whenever we repeat an experiment a large number of times (for example, measuring somebody's height), the distribution of results can be approximated by a Gaussian.

Generally, we have a multivariate (that is, involving more than one feature) distribution, but the idea is the same. There is a point in the hyperplane (the mean) most instances will be closer to; when we move away from the mean, the probability of finding a point in the cluster will decrease. How far this probability decreases is dependent on the second parameter, the variance. As we said, GMM assumes each cluster has a multivariate normal distribution, and the method objective is to find the k centroids (estimating mean and variance from training data using an algorithm called **Expectation-Maximization (EM)**) and assign each point to the nearest mean. Let's see how it works on our example.

```
>>> from sklearn import mixture
>>> gm = mixture.GMM(n_components=n_digits,
    covariance_type='tied', random_state=42)
>>> gm.fit(X_train)
GMM(covariance_type='tied', init_params='wmc', min_covar=0.001,n_
components=10, n_init=1, n_iter=100, params='wmc',random_
state=42,thresh=0.01)
```

You can observe that the procedure is exactly the same as the one we used for k-means. `covariance_type` is a method parameter that indicates how we expect features; that is, each pixel to be related. For example, we can suppose that they are independent, but we can also expect that closer points are correlated, and so on. For the moment, we will use the tied covariance type. In the next chapter, we will show some techniques to select between different parameter values.

Let's see how it performs on our testing data:

```
>>> # Print train clustering and confusion matrix
>>> y_pred = gm.predict(X_test)
>>> print "Adjusted rand
    score:{:.2}".format(metrics.adjusted_rand_score(y_test,
    y_pred))
Adjusted rand score:0.65

>>> print "Homogeneity score:{:.2}
    ".format(metrics.homogeneity_score(y_test, y_pred))
Homogeneity score:0.74

>>> print "Completeness score: {:.2}
    ".format(metrics.completeness_score(y_test, y_pred))
Completeness score: 0.79
```

Compared to k-means, we achieved a better Rand score (0.65 versus 0.59), indicating that we have better aligned our clusters with the original digits. We also included two interesting measures included in `sklearn.metrics`. **Homogeneity** is a number between 0.0 and 1.0 (greater is better). A value of 1.0 indicates that clusters only contain data points from a single class; that is, clusters effectively group similar instances. **Completeness**, on the other hand, is satisfied when every data point of a given class is within the same cluster (meaning that we have grouped all possible instances of the class, instead of building several uniform but smaller clusters). We can see homogeneity and completeness as the unsupervised versions of precision and recall.

Summary

In this chapter we presented some of the most important unsupervised learning methods. We did not intend to provide you with an exhaustive introduction to all the possible methods, but instead a brief introduction to these kinds of techniques. We described how we can use unsupervised algorithms to perform a quick data analysis to understand the behavior of the dataset and also perform dimensionality reduction. Both applications are very useful as a step before applying a supervised learning method. We also applied unsupervised learning techniques such as k-means to resolve problems without using a target class—a very useful way to create applications on top of untagged data.

In *Chapter 4*, *Advanced Features*, we will look at techniques that will allow us to obtain better results in the application of machine learning algorithms. We will look at data-preprocessing and feature-selection techniques to obtain better features to learn from. Also, we will use grid search techniques to obtain the parameters that produce the best performance with our algorithms.

4
Advanced Features

In the previous chapters we have studied several algorithms for very different tasks, from classification and regression to clustering and dimensionality reduction. We showed how we can apply these algorithms to predict results when faced with new data. That is what machine learning is all about. In this last chapter, we want to show some important concepts and methods you should take into account if you want to do real-world machine learning.

- In real-world problems, usually data is not already expressed by attribute/ float value pairs, but through more complex structures or is not structured at all. We will learn **feature extraction** techniques that will allow us to extract scikit-learn features from data.

- From the initial set of available features, not all of them will be useful for our algorithms to learn from; in fact, some of them may degrade our performance. We will address the problem of selecting the most adequate feature set, a process known as **feature selection**.

- Finally, as we have seen in the examples in this book, many of the machine learning algorithms have parameters that must be set in order to use them. To do that, we will review **model selection** techniques; that is, methods to select the most promising hyperparameters to our algorithms.

All these steps are crucial in order to obtain decent results when working with machine learning applications.

Feature extraction

The usual scenario for learning tasks such as those presented in this book include a list of instances (represented as feature/value pairs) and a special feature (the target class) that we want to predict for future instances based on the values of the remaining features. However, the source data does not usually come in this format. We have to extract what we think are potentially useful features and convert them to our learning format. This process is called feature extraction or feature engineering, and it is an often underestimated but very important and time-consuming phase in most real-world machine learning tasks. We can identify two different steps in this task:

- **Obtain features**: This step involves processing the source data and extracting the learning instances, usually in the form of feature/value pairs where the value can be an integer or float value, a string, a categorical value, and so on. The method used for extraction depends heavily on how the data is presented. For example, we can have a set of pictures and generate an integer-valued feature for each pixel, indicating its color level, as we did in the face recognition example in *Chapter 2, Supervised Learning*. Since this is a very task-dependent job, we will not delve into details and assume we already have this setting for our examples.

- **Convert features**: Most scikit-learn algorithms assume as an input a set of instances represented as a list of float-valued features. How to get these features will be the main subject of this section.

We can, as we did in *Chapter 2, Supervised Learning*, build ad hoc procedures to convert the source data. There are, however, tools that can help us to obtain a suitable representation. The Python package pandas (http://pandas.pydata.org/), for example, provides data structures and tools for data analysis. It aims to provide similar features to those of R, the popular language and environment for statistical computing. We will use pandas to import the Titanic data we presented in *Chapter 2, Supervised Learning*, and convert them to the scikit-learn format.

Let's start by importing the original titanic.csv data into a pandas DataFrame data structure (DataFrame is essentially a two-dimensional labeled data structure where columns can potentially include different data types and each row represents an instance). As usual, we previously import the numpy and pyplot packages.

```
>>> %pylab inline
>>> import pandas as pd
>>> import numpy as np
>>> import matplotlib.pyplot as plt
```

Then we import the Titanic data with pandas.

```
>>> titanic = pd.read_csv('data/titanic.csv')
>>> print titanic
<class 'pandas.core.frame.DataFrame'>
Int64Index: 1313 entries, 0 to 1312
Data columns (total 11 columns):
row.names    1313  non-null values
pclass       1313  non-null values
survived     1313  non-null values
name         1313  non-null values
age          633   non-null values
embarked     821   non-null values
home.dest    754   non-null values
room         77    non-null values
ticket       69    non-null values
boat         347   non-null values
sex          1313  non-null values
dtypes: float64(1), int64(2), object(8)
```

You can see that each csv column has a corresponding feature into the DataFrame, and that the feature type is induced from the available data. We can inspect some features to see what they look like.

```
>>> print titanic.head()[['pclass', 'survived', 'age', 'embarked',
       'boat', 'sex']]
   pclass  survived      age    embarked  boat     sex
0  1st          1   29.0000  Southampton    2  female
1  1st          0    2.0000  Southampton  NaN  female
2  1st          0   30.0000  Southampton (135)    male
3  1st          0   25.0000  Southampton  NaN  female
4  1st          1    0.9167  Southampton   11    male
```

The main difficulty we have now is that scikit-learn methods expect real numbers as feature values. In *Chapter 2, Supervised Learning*, we used the `LabelEncoder` and `OneHotEncoder` preprocessing methods to manually convert certain categorical features into 1-of-K values (generating a new feature for each possible value; valued `1` if the original feature had the corresponding value and `0` otherwise). This time, we will use a similar scikit-learn method, `DictVectorizer`, which automatically builds these features from the different original feature values. Moreover, we will program a method to encode a set of columns in a unique step.

```
>>> from sklearn import feature_extraction
>>> def one_hot_dataframe(data, cols, replace=False):
>>>     vec = feature_extraction.DictVectorizer()
>>>     mkdict = lambda row: dict((col, row[col]) for col in cols)
>>>     vecData = pd.DataFrame(vec.fit_transform(
>>>         data[cols].apply(mkdict, axis=1)).toarray())
>>>     vecData.columns = vec.get_feature_names()
>>>     vecData.index = data.index
>>>     if replace:
>>>         data = data.drop(cols, axis=1)
>>>         data = data.join(vecData)
>>>     return (data, vecData)
```

The `one_hot_dataframe` method (based on the script at `https://gist.github.com/kljensen/5452382`) takes a pandas `DataFrame` data structure and a list of columns and encodes each column into the necessary 1-of-K features. If the `replace` parameter is `True`, it will also substitute the original column with the new set. Let's see it applied to the categorical `pclass`, `embarked`, and `sex` features (`titanic_n` only contains the previously created columns):

```
>>> titanic,titanic_n = one_hot_dataframe(titanic, ['pclass',
    'embarked', 'sex'], replace=True)
>>> titanic.describe()
<class 'pandas.core.frame.DataFrame'>
Index: 8 entries, count to max
Data columns (total 12 columns):
row.names               8   non-null values
survived                8   non-null values
age                     8   non-null values
embarked                8   non-null values
embarked=Cherbourg      8   non-null values
embarked=Queenstown     8   non-null values
embarked=Southampton    8   non-null values
pclass=1st              8   non-null values
pclass=2nd              8   non-null values
pclass=3rd              8   non-null values
sex=female              8   non-null values
sex=male                8   non-null values
dtypes: float64(12)
```

The `pclass` attribute has been converted to three `pclass=1st`, `pclass=2nd`, `pclass=3rd` features, and similarly for the other two features. Note that the `embarked` feature has not disappeared, This is due to the fact that the original `embarked` attribute included `NaN` values, indicating a missing value; in those cases, every feature based on embarked will be valued `0`, but the original feature whose value is `NaN` remains, indicating the feature is missing for certain instances. Next, we encode the remaining categorical attributes:

```
>>> titanic, titanic_n = one_hot_dataframe(titanic, ['home.dest',
    'room', 'ticket', 'boat'], replace=True)
```

We also have to deal with missing values, since `DecisionTreeClassifier` we plan to use does not admit them on input. Pandas allow us to replace them with a fixed value using the `fillna` method. We will use the mean age for the `age` feature, and `0` for the remaining missing attributes.

```
>>> mean = titanic['age'].mean()
>>> titanic['age'].fillna(mean, inplace=True)
>>> titanic.fillna(0, inplace=True)
```

Now, all of our features (except for `Name`) are in a suitable format. We are ready to build the test and training sets, as usual.

```
>>> from sklearn.cross_validation import train_test_split
>>> titanic_target = titanic['survived']
>>> titanic_data = titanic.drop(['name', 'row.names', 'survived'],
    axis=1)
>>> X_train, X_test, y_train, y_test =
    train_test_split(titanic_data, titanic_target, test_size=0.25,
    random_state=33)
```

We decided to simply drop the `name` attribute, since we do not expect it to be informative about the survival status (we have one different value for each instance, so we can generalize over it). We also specified the `survived` feature as the target class, and consequently eliminated it from the training vector.

Let's see how a decision tree works with the current feature set.

```
>>> from sklearn import tree
>>> dt = tree.DecisionTreeClassifier(criterion='entropy')
>>> dt = dt.fit(X_train, y_train)
>>> from sklearn import metrics
>>> y_pred = dt.predict(X_test)
>>> print "Accuracy:{0:.3f}".format(metrics.accuracy_score(y_test,
    y_pred)), "\n"
Accuracy:0.839
```

Feature selection

Until now, when training our decision tree, we used every available feature in our learning dataset. This seems perfectly reasonable, since we want to use as much information as there is available to build our model. There are, however, two main reasons why we would want to restrict the number of features used:

- Firstly, for some methods, especially those (such as decision trees) that reduce the number of instances used to refine the model at each step, it is possible that irrelevant features could suggest correlations between features and target classes that arise just by chance and do not correctly model the problem. This aspect is also related to overfitting; having certain over-specific features may lead to poor generalization. Besides, some features may be highly correlated, and will simply add redundant information.

- The second reason is a real-world one. A large number of features could greatly increase the computation time without a corresponding classifier improvement. This is of particular importance when working with Big Data, where the number of instances and features could easily grow to several thousand or more. Also, in relation to the curse of dimensionality, learning a generalizable model from a dataset with too many features relative to the number of instances can be difficult.

As a result, working with a smaller feature set may lead to better results. So we want to find some way to algorithmically find the best features. This task is called feature selection and is a crucial step when we aim to get decent results with machine learning algorithms. If we have poor features, our algorithm will return poor results no matter how sophisticated our machine learning algorithm is.

Consider, for example, our very simple Titanic example. We started with just 11 features, but after 1-of-K encoding they grew to 581.

```
>>> print titanic
<class 'pandas.core.frame.DataFrame'> Int64Index: 1313 entries, 0
to 1312 Columns: 581 entries, row.names to ticket=L15 1s dtypes:
float64(578), int64(2), object(1)
```

This does not pose an important computational problem, but consider what could happen if, as previously demonstrated, we represent each document in a dataset as the number of occurrences of each possible word. Another problem is that decision trees suffer from overfitting. If branching is based on a very small number of instances, the prediction power of the built model will decrease on future data. One solution to this is to adjust model parameters (such as the maximum tree depth or the minimum required number of instances at a leaf node). In this example, however, we will take a different approach: we will try to limit the features to the most relevant ones.

What do we mean by relevant? This is an important question. A general approach is to find the smallest set of features that correctly characterize the training data. If a feature always coincides with the target class (that is, it is a perfect predictor), it is enough to characterize the data. On the other hand, if a feature always has the same value, its prediction power will be very low.

The general approach in feature selection is to get some kind of evaluation function that, when given a potential feature, returns a score of how useful the feature is, and then keeps the features with the highest scores. These methods may have the disadvantage of not detecting correlations between features. Other methods may be more brute force: try all possible subsets of the original feature list, train the algorithm on each combination, and keep the combination that gets the best results.

As an evaluation method, we can, for instance, use a statistical test that measures how probable it is that two random variables (say, a given feature and the target class) are independent; that is, there is no correlation between them.

Scikit-learn provides several methods in the `feature_selection` module. We will use the `SelectPercentile` method that, when given a statistical test, selects a user-specified percentile of features with the highest scoring. The most popular statistical test is the χ^2 (chi-squared) statistic. Let's see how it works for our Titanic example; we will use it to select 20 percent of the most important features:

```
>>> from sklearn import feature_selection
>>> fs = feature_selection.SelectPercentile(
        feature_selection.chi2, percentile=20)
>>> X_train_fs = fs.fit_transform(X_train, y_train)
```

The `X_train_fs` array now has the statistically more important features. We can now train our decision tree on this data.

```
>>> dt.fit(X_train_fs, y_train)
>>> X_test_fs = fs.transform(X_test)
>>> y_pred_fs = dt.predict(X_test_fs)
>>> print "Accuracy:{0:.3f}".format(metrics.accuracy_score(y_test,
    y_pred_fs)),"\n"
Accuracy:0.845
```

We can see that the accuracy on the training set improved half a point after feature selection on the training set.

Is it possible to find the optimal number of features? If by optimal we mean with the best performance on the training set, it is actually possible; we can simply use a brute-force approach and try with different numbers of features while measuring their performance on the training set using cross-validation.

```
>>> from sklearn import cross_validation
>>>
>>> percentiles = range(1, 100, 5)
>>> results = []
>>> for i in range(1,100,5):
>>>     fs = feature_selection.SelectPercentile(
            feature_selection.chi2, percentile=i
        )
>>>     X_train_fs = fs.fit_transform(X_train, y_train)
>>>     scores = cross_validation.cross_val_score(dt, X_train_fs,
        y_train, cv=5)
>>>     results = np.append(results, scores.mean())
>>> optimal_percentil = np.where(results == results.max())[0]
>>> print "Optimal number of features:{0}".format(
        percentiles[optimal_percentil]), "\n"
Optimal number of features:11
>>>
>>> # Plot number of features VS. cross-validation scores
>>> import pylab as pl
>>> pl.figure()
>>> pl.xlabel("Number of features selected")
>>> pl.ylabel("Cross-validation accuracy)")
>>> pl.plot(percentiles, results)
```

The following figure shows how cross-validation accuracy changes with the number of features:

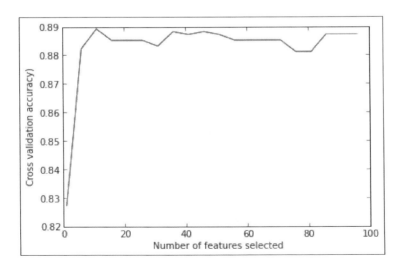

We can see that accuracy quickly improves when we start adding features, remaining stable after the percentile of features turns about 10. In fact, the best accuracy is achieved when using 64 of the original 581 features (at the 11 percent percentile). Let's see if this actually improved performance on the testing set.

```
>>> fs = feature_selection.SelectPercentile(
            feature_selection.chi2,
            percentile=percentiles[optimal_percentil])
>>> X_train_fs = fs.fit_transform(X_train, y_train)
>>> dt.fit(X_train_fs, y_train)
>>> X_test_fs = fs.transform(X_test)
>>> y_pred_fs = dt.predict(X_test_fs)
>>> print "Accuracy:{0:.3f}".format(metrics.accuracy_score(y_test,
    y_pred_fs)), "\n"
Accuracy:0.848
```

The performance improved slightly, again. Compared with our initial performance, we have finally improved by almost one accuracy point using only 11 percent of the features.

The reader may have noted that while creating our classifier, we used the default parameters, except for the splitting criterion, where we have used `entropy`. Can we improve our model using different parameters? This task is called model selection, and we will address it in detail in the next section using a different learning example. For now, let's just test if the alternative method (`gini`) would result in better performance for our example. To do this, we will again use cross-validation.

```
>>> dt = tree.DecisionTreeClassifier(criterion='entropy')
>>> scores = cross_validation.cross_val_score(dt, X_train_fs,
    y_train, cv=5)
>>> print "Entropy criterion accuracy on
    cv: {0:.3f}".format(scores.mean())
Entropy criterion accuracy on cv: 0.889
>>> dt = tree.DecisionTreeClassifier(criterion='gini')
>>> scores = cross_validation.cross_val_score(dt, X_train_fs,
    y_train, cv=5)
>>> print "Gini criterion accuracy on
    cv: {0:.3f}".format(scores.mean())
Gini criterion accuracy on cv: 0.897
```

The Gini criterion performs better on our training set. How about its performance on the test set?

```
>>> dt.fit(X_train_fs, y_train)
>>> X_test_fs = fs.transform(X_test)
>>> y_pred_fs = dt.predict(X_test_fs)
>>> print "Accuracy:
    {0:.3f}".format(metrics.accuracy_score(y_test,
    y_pred_fs)),"\n"
Accuracy: 0.848
```

It seems that performance improvement on the training set did not hold for the evaluation set. This is always possible. In fact, performance could have decreased (recall overfitting). Our model is still the best. If we changed our model to use the one with the best performance in the testing set, we can never measure its performance, since the testing dataset could not be considered "unseen data" anymore.

Model selection

In the previous section we worked on ways to preprocess the data and select the most promising features. As we stated, selecting a good set of features is a crucial step to obtain good results. Now we will focus on another important step: selecting the algorithm parameters, known as **hyperparameters** to distinguish them from the parameters that are adjusted within the machine learning algorithm. Many machine learning algorithms include hyperparameters (from now on we will simply call them parameters) that guide certain aspects of the underlying method and have great impact on the results. In this section we will review some methods to help us obtain the best parameter configuration, a process known as model selection.

We will look back at the text-classification problem we addressed in *Chapter 2, Supervised Learning*. In that example, we compounded a TF-IDF vectorizer alongside a multinomial **Naïve Bayes (NB)** algorithm to classify a set of newsgroup messages into a discrete number of categories. The MultinomialNB algorithm has one important parameter, named alpha, that adjusts the smoothing. We initially used the class with its default parameter values (alpha = 1.0) and obtained an accuracy of 0.89. But when we set alpha to 0.01, we obtained a noticeable accuracy improvement to 0.92. Clearly, the configuration of the alpha parameter has great impact on the performance of the algorithm. How can we be sure 0.01 is the best value? Perhaps if we try other possible values, we could still obtain better results.

Let's start again with our text-classification problem, but for now we will only use a reduced number of instances. We will work only with 3,000 instances. We start by importing our `pylab` environment and loading the data.

```
>>> %pylab inline
>>> from sklearn.datasets import fetch_20newsgroups
>>> news = fetch_20newsgroups(subset='all')
>>> n_samples = 3000
>>> X_train = news.data[:n_samples]
>>> y_train = news.target[:n_samples]
```

After that, we need to import the classes to construct our classifier.

```
>>> from sklearn.naive_bayes import MultinomialNB
>>> from sklearn.pipeline import Pipeline
>>> from sklearn.feature_extraction.text import TfidfVectorizer
```

Then import the set of stop words and create a pipeline that compounds the TF-IDF vectorizer and the Naïve Bayes algorithms (recall that we had a `stopwords_en.txt` file with a list of stop words).

```
>>> def get_stop_words():
>>>     result = set()
>>>     for line in open('stopwords_en.txt', 'r').readlines():
>>>         result.add(line.strip())
>>>     return result
>>> stop_words = get_stop_words()
>>> clf = Pipeline([('vect', TfidfVectorizer(
>>>         stop_words=stop_words,
>>>         token_pattern=ur"\b[a-z0-9_\-\.]+[a-z][a-z0-9_\-
>>>         \.]+\b",
>>>     )),
>>>     ('nb', MultinomialNB(alpha=0.01)),
>>>])
```

If we evaluate our algorithm with a three-fold cross-validation, we obtain a mean score of around 0.811.

```
>>> from sklearn.cross_validation import cross_val_score, KFold
>>> from scipy.stats import sem
>>> def evaluate_cross_validation(clf, X, y, K):
>>>     # create a k-fold croos validation iterator of k=5 folds
>>>     cv = KFold(len(y), K, shuffle=True, random_state=0)
>>>     # by default the score used is the one returned by score
        method of the estimator (accuracy)
>>>     scores = cross_val_score(clf, X, y, cv=cv)
>>>     print scores
>>>     print ("Mean score: {0:.3f} (+/-{1:.3f})").format(
>>>         np.mean(scores), sem(scores))
>>> evaluate_cross_validation(clf, X_train, y_train, 3)
[ 0.814  0.815  0.804]
Mean score: 0.811 (+/-0.004)
```

It looks like we should train the algorithm with a list of different parameter values and keep the parameter value that achieves the best results. Let's implement a helper function to do that. This function will train the algorithm with a list of values, each time obtaining an accuracy score calculated by performing k-fold cross-validation on the training instances. After that, it will plot the training and testing scores as a function of the parameter values.

```
>>> def calc_params(X, y, clf, param_values, param_name, K):
>>>     # initialize training and testing scores with zeros
>>>     train_scores = np.zeros(len(param_values))
>>>     test_scores = np.zeros(len(param_values))
>>>
>>>     # iterate over the different parameter values
>>>     for i, param_value in enumerate(param_values):
>>>         print param_name, ' = ', param_value
>>>         # set classifier parameters
>>>         clf.set_params(**{param_name:param_value})
>>>         # initialize the K scores obtained for each fold
>>>         k_train_scores = np.zeros(K)
>>>         k_test_scores = np.zeros(K)
>>>         # create KFold cross validation
>>>         cv = KFold(n_samples, K, shuffle=True, random_state=0)
>>>         # iterate over the K folds
```

```
>>>         for j, (train, test) in enumerate(cv):
>>>             clf.fit([X[k] for k in train], y[train])
>>>             k_train_scores[j] = clf.score([X[k] for k in
                train], y[train])
>>>             k_test_scores[j] = clf.score([X[k] for k in test],
                y[test])
>>>         train_scores[i] = np.mean(k_train_scores)
>>>         test_scores[i] = np.mean(k_test_scores)
>>>
>>>     # plot the training and testing scores in a log scale
>>>     plt.semilogx(param_values, train_scores, alpha=0.4, lw=2,
            c='b')
>>>     plt.semilogx(param_values, test_scores, alpha=0.4, lw=2,
            c='g')
>>>     plt.xlabel("Alpha values")
>>>     plt.ylabel("Mean cross-validation accuracy")
>>>     # return the training and testing scores on each parameter
        value
>>>     return train_scores, test_scores
```

The function accepts six arguments: the feature array, the target array, the classifier object to be used, the list of parameter values, the name of the parameter to adjust, and the number of K folds to be used in the crossvalidation evaluation.

Let's call this function; we will use numpy's `logspace` function to generate a list of alpha values spaced evenly on a log scale.

```
>>> alphas = np.logspace(-7, 0, 8)
>>> print alphas
[  1.00000000e-07   1.00000000e-06   1.00000000e-05   1.00000000e-04
   1.00000000e-03   1.00000000e-02   1.00000000e-01   1.00000000e+00]
```

We will set the values of the `alpha` parameter of the NB classifier within the pipeline, which corresponds to the parameter name `nb__alpha`. We will use three folds for the cross-validation.

```
>>> train_scores, test_scores = calc_params(X_train, y_train, clf,
alphas, 'nb__alpha', 3)
```

In the following figure, the line at the top corresponds to the training accuracy and the one at the bottom to the testing accuracy:

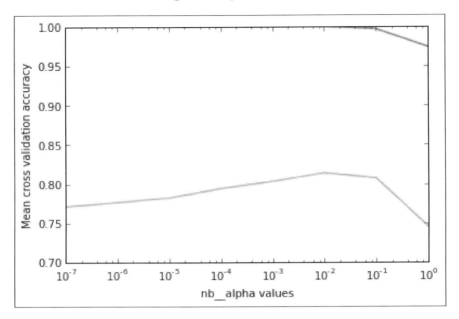

As expected, the training accuracy is always greater than the testing accuracy. We can see in the graph that the best testing accuracy is obtained with an alpha value in the range of 10^{-2} and 10^{-1}. Below this range, the classifier shows signs of overfitting (the training accuracy is high but the testing accuracy is lower than it could be). Above this range, the classifier shows signs of underfitting (accuracy on the training set is lower than it could be).

It is worth mentioning that at this point a second pass could be performed in the range of 10-2 and 10-1with a finer grid to find an ever better alpha value.

Let's print the scores vector to look at the actual values.

```
>>> print 'training scores: ', train_scores
>>> print 'testing scores: ', test_scores
training scores:  [ 1. 1. 1. 1. 1. 0.99933333 0.99633333 0.96933333]
testing scores:  [ 0.75 0.75666667 0.76433333 0.77533333 0.78866667
0.811 0.81233333 0.753]
```

The best results are obtained with an `alpha` value of `0.1` (accuracy of 0.812).

We created a very useful function to graph and obtain the best parameter value for a classifier. Let's use it to adjust another classifier that uses a **Support Vector Machines (SVM)** instead of `MultinomialNB`:

```
>>> from sklearn.svm import SVC
>>>
>>> clf = Pipeline([
>>>     ('vect', TfidfVectorizer(
>>>                 stop_words=stop_words,
>>>                 token_pattern=ur"\b[a-z0-9_\-\.]+[a-z][a-z0-
>>>                 9_\-\.]+\b",
>>>     )),
>>>     ('svc', SVC()),
>>> ])
```

We created a pipeline as before, but now we use the SVC classifier with its default values. Now we will use our `calc_params` function to adjust the `gamma` parameter.

```
>>> gammas = np.logspace(-2, 1, 4)
>>> train_scores, test_scores = calc_params(X_train, y_train, clf,
gammas,'svc__gamma', 3)
```

For gamma values lesser than one we have underfitting and for gamma values greater than one we have overfitting.

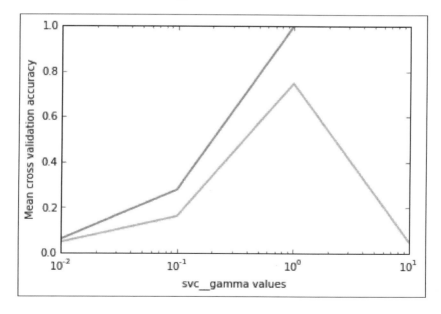

So the best result is for a `gamma` value of `1`, where we obtain a training accuracy of 0.999 and a testing accuracy of 0.760.

If you take a closer look at the SVC class constructor parameters, we have other parameters, apart from gamma, that may also affect classifier performance. If we only adjust the gamma value, we implicitly state that the optimal `C` value is `1.0` (the default value that we did not explicitly set). Perhaps we could obtain better results with a new combination of `C` and `gamma` values. This opens a new degree of complexity; we should try all the parameter combinations and keep the better one.

Grid search

To mitigate this problem, we have a very useful class named `GridSearchCV` within the `sklearn.grid_search` module. What we have been doing with our `calc_params` function is a kind of grid search in one dimension. With `GridSearchCV`, we can specify a grid of any number of parameters and parameter values to traverse. It will train the classifier for each combination and obtain a cross-validation accuracy to evaluate each one.

Let's use it to adjust the `C` and the `gamma` parameters at the same time.

```
>>> from sklearn.grid_search import GridSearchCV

>>> parameters = {
>>>     'svc__gamma': np.logspace(-2, 1, 4),
>>>     'svc__C': np.logspace(-1, 1, 3),
>>> }
>>> clf = Pipeline([
>>>     ('vect', TfidfVectorizer(
>>>             stop_words=stop_words,
>>>             token_pattern=ur"\b[a-z0-9_\-\.]+[a-z][a-z0-
                9_\-\.]+\b",
>>>     )),
>>>     ('svc', SVC()),
>>> ])
>>> gs = GridSearchCV(clf, parameters, verbose=2, refit=False, cv=3)
```

Let's execute our grid search and print the best parameter values and scores.

```
>>> %time _ = gs.fit(X_train, y_train)
>>> gs.best_params_, gs.best_score_
CPU times: user 304.39 s, sys: 2.55 s, total: 306.94 s
Wall time: 306.56 s
  ({'svc__C': 10.0, 'svc__gamma': 0.10000000000000001},
0.81166666666666665)
```

With the grid search, we obtained a better combination of C and gamma parameters, for values 10.0 and 0.10 respectively, with a three-fold cross-validation accuracy of 0.811, which is much better than the best value we obtained (0.76) in the previous experiment by only adjusting gamma and keeping the C value at 1.0.

At this point, we could continue performing experiments by trying not only to adjust other parameters of the SVC but also adjusting the parameters on TfidfVectorizer, which is also part of the estimator. Note that this additionally increases the complexity. As you might have noticed, the previous grid search experiment took about five minutes to finish. If we add new parameters to adjust, the time will increase exponentially. As a result, these kinds of methods are very resource/time intensive; this is also the reason why we used only a subset of the total instances.

Parallel grid search

Grid search calculation grows exponentially with each parameter and its possible values we want to tune. We could reduce our response time if we calculate each of the combinations in parallel instead of sequentially, as we have done. In our previous example, we had four different values for gamma and three different values for C, summing up 12 parameter combinations. Additionally, we also needed to train each combination three times (in a three-fold cross-validation), so we summed up 36 trainings and evaluations. We could try to run these 36 tasks in parallel, since the tasks are independent.

Most modern computers have multiple cores that can be used to run tasks in parallel. We also have a very useful tool within IPython, called **IPython parallel**, that allows us to run independent tasks in parallel, each task in a different core of our machine. Let's do that with our text classifier example.

We will first declare a function that will persist all K folds for the cross-validation in different files. These files will be loaded by a process that will execute the corresponding fold. To do that, we will use the joblib library.

```
>>> from sklearn.externals import joblib
>>> from sklearn.cross_validation import ShuffleSplit
>>> import os
>>> def persist_cv_splits(X, y, K=3, name='data',
                          suffix="_cv_%03d.pkl"):
>>>     """Dump K folds to filesystem."""
>>>
>>>     cv_split_filenames = []
>>>
```

```
>>>     # create KFold cross validation
>>>     cv = KFold(n_samples, K, shuffle=True, random_state=0)
>>>
>>>     # iterate over the K folds
>>>     for i, (train, test) in enumerate(cv):
>>>         cv_fold = ([X[k] for k in train], y[train], [X[k] for
>>>                     k in test], y[test])
>>>         cv_split_filename = name + suffix % i
>>>         cv_split_filename = os.path.abspath(cv_split_filename)
>>>         joblib.dump(cv_fold, cv_split_filename)
>>>         cv_split_filenames.append(cv_split_filename)
>>>
>>>     return cv_split_filenames
>>> cv_filenames = persist_cv_splits(X, y, name='news')
```

The following function loads a particular fold and fits the classifier with the specified parameter set, returning the testing score. This function will be called by each of the parallel tasks.

```
>>> def compute_evaluation(cv_split_filename, clf, params):
>>>
>>>     # All module imports should be executed in the worker
        namespace
>>>     from sklearn.externals import joblib
>>>
>>>     # load the fold training and testing partitions from the
        filesystem
>>>     X_train, y_train, X_test, y_test = joblib.load(
>>>         cv_split_filename, mmap_mode='c')
>>>
>>>     clf.set_params(**params)
>>>     clf.fit(X_train, y_train)
>>>     test_score = clf.score(X_test, y_test)
>>>     return test_score
```

Finally, the following function executes the grid search in parallel tasks. For each parameter combination (returned by the `IterGrid` iterator), it iterates over K folds and creates a task to compute the evaluation. It returns the parameter combinations alongside the tasks list.

```
>>> from sklearn.grid_search import IterGrid
>>>
>>> def parallel_grid_search(lb_view, clf, cv_split_filenames, param_
grid):
>>>     all_tasks = []
>>>     all_parameters = list(IterGrid(param_grid))
>>>
>>>     # iterate over parameter combinations
>>>     for i, params in enumerate(all_parameters):
>>>         task_for_params = []
>>>         # iterate over the K folds
>>>         for j, cv_split_filename in
                enumerate(cv_split_filenames):
>>>             t = lb_view.apply(
>>>                 compute_evaluation, cv_split_filename, clf,
                    params)
>>>             task_for_params.append(t)
>>>
>>>         all_tasks.append(task_for_params)
>>>
>>>     return all_parameters, all_tasks
```

Now we use IPython parallel to get the client and a load balanced view. We must first create a local cluster of N engines (one for each core of your machine) using the `Cluster` tab in the IPython Notebook. Then we create the client and the view and execute our `parallel_grid_search` function.

```
>>> from sklearn.svm import SVC
>>> from IPython.parallel import Client
>>>
>>> client = Client()
>>> lb_view = client.load_balanced_view()
>>>
>>> all_parameters, all_tasks = parallel_grid_search(
    lb_view, clf, cv_filenames, parameters)
```

IPython parallel will start to run the tasks in parallel. We can use this to monitor the progress of the whole task group.

```
>>> def print_progress(tasks):
>>>     progress = np.mean([task.ready() for task_group in tasks
                              for task in task_group])
>>>     print "Tasks completed: {0}%".format(100 * progress)
```

After all the tasks are completed, use the following function:

```
>>> print_progress(all_tasks)
Tasks completed: 100.0%
```

We can define a function that computes the mean score of the completed tasks.

```
>>> def find_bests(all_parameters, all_tasks, n_top=5):
>>>     """Compute the mean score of the completed tasks"""
>>>     mean_scores = []
>>>
>>>     for param, task_group in zip(all_parameters, all_tasks):
>>>         scores = [t.get() for t in task_group if t.ready()]
>>>         if len(scores) == 0:
>>>             continue
>>>         mean_scores.append((np.mean(scores), param))
>>>
>>>     return sorted(mean_scores, reverse=True)[:n_top]
>>> print find_bests(all_parameters, all_tasks)

[(0.81733333333333336, {'svc__gamma': 0.1000000000000001, 'svc__C':
10.0}), (0.78733333333333333, {'svc__gamma': 1.0, 'svc__C':
10.0}), (0.76000000000000012, {'svc__gamma': 1.0, 'svc__C': 1.0}),
(0.30099999999999999, {'svc__gamma': 0.01, 'svc__C': 10.0}),
(0.19933333333333333, {'svc__gamma': 0.1000000000000001, 'svc__C':
1.0})]
```

You can observe that we computed the same results as in the previous section, but in half the time (if you used two cores) or in a quarter of the time (if you used four cores).

Summary

In this chapter we reviewed two important methods to improve our results when applying machine learning algorithms: feature selection and model selection. First, we used different techniques to preprocess data, extract features, and select the most promising features. Then we used techniques to automatically calculate the most promising hyperparameters of machine learning algorithms and used methods to parallelize these calculations.

The reader must be aware that this book covered only the main machine learning lines and some of their methods. Keep in mind that there is much more than supervised and unsupervised learning. For example:

- Semi-supervised learning methods are the middle ground between supervised and unsupervised learning. They combine small amounts of annotated data with huge amounts of unlabeled data. Usually, unlabeled data can reveal the underlying distribution of elements and obtain better results in combination with a small, labeled dataset.

- Active learning is a particular case within semi-supervised methods. Again, it is useful when labeled data is scarce or hard to obtain. In active learning, the algorithm actively queries a human expert to answer the label of certain unlabeled instances, and thus learn the concept over a reduced set of labeled instances.

- Reinforcement learning proposes methods where an agent learns from feedback (rewards or reinforcements) after performing actions within an environment. The agent learns to perform a task by trying to maximize the cumulative reward. These methods have been very successful in robotics and video games.

- Sequential classification (very commonly used in **Natural Language Processing (NLP)**) assigns a sequence of labels to a sequence of items; for example, the parts of speech of the words in a sentence.

Besides these, there are lots of supervised learning methods with radically different approaches to those we presented; for example, neural networks, maximum entropy models, memory-based models, and rule-based models. Machine learning is a very active research area with a growing literature; there are many books and courses that the reader can use to go deeper into the theory and details.

Scikit-learn has many of these algorithms implemented, and lacks others, but expect its active and enthusiastic contributors to build them soon. We encourage the reader to be part of the community!

Index

G

Gaussian Mixture Models (GMM) 61, 75
Graphviz
  URL 48
grid search
  about 94, 95
  parallel grid search 95-98

H

harmonic mean 17
HashingVectorizer 36
Homogeneity 77
house prices
  linear model 55, 56
  performance, evaluating 59
  predicting, with regression 53, 54
  Random Forests 58
  Support Vector Machines 57

I

image recognition
  with Support Vector Machines 25-28
Information Gain (IG) 48, 49
intercept_ attribute 13
IPython Notebook 6
IPython parallel 95
IterGrid iterator 97

K

k-means 61, 67

L

labels_ attribute 69
Large Hadron Collider. *See* **LHC**
Law of Large Numbers 75
leave-one-out cross-validation 50
LHC 25
linear classification 10-15
Linux
  Scikit-learn, installing on 7

M

Mac
  Scikit-learn, installing on 8
machine learning
  concepts 21, 22
  issues 6
  linear classification 10-15
  method 10-13
  results, evaluating 16-20
machine learning categories 20
matplotlib package
  URL, for installing 6
measure_performance function 59
meshgrid
  of points 72
model selection 51, 79, 88, 90-94
MultinomialNB algorithm 88

N

Naïve Bayes
  about 33
  classifier, training 36-39
  data, preprocessing 35, 36
  performance, evaluating 40
  used, for classifying text 33, 35
Natural Language Processing. *See* **NLP**
n-init parameter 69
NLP 34
NumPy
  URL 6

O

one_hot_dataframe method 82
OneHotEncoder class 47
one hot encoding 46
overfitting 16

P

parallel_grid_search function 97
PCA
  about 62-66
  feature, selecting 63
  function, defining 64
  visualization 62
pclass attribute 83
Pipeline class 19
precision 17
Principal Component Analysis. *See* PCA
print_digits function 68, 74
print_faces function 31
pydot module 48
Python package pandas
  URL 80

R

Rand index 71
Random Forests 51
recall 17
replace parameter 82

S

Scikit-learn
  about 6, 25
  installation, checking 8
  installing 6
  installing, on Linux 7
  installing, on Mac 8
  installing, on Windows 8
  tutorial, URL 72
SciPy
  URL 6
SelectPercentile method 85
SGD 13
SGDClassifier initialization function 13
sklearn.datasets module 34
sklearn.decomposition module 64
sklearn.ensemble module 52, 58
sklearn.feature_extraction.text
    module 35, 36

sklearn.grid_search module 94
sklearn.naive_bayes module 36
sklearn.pipeline module 36
sklearn.svm module 28
spam filtering 34
Stochastic Gradient Descent. *See* SGD
supervised learning algorithm 25
survived feature 83
SVC
  about 29-31
  data, reshaping 33
  image recognition with 25-28
  training 28

T

target array 9
Term Frequency Inverse Document
    Frequency (TF-IDF) 36
TfidfVectorizer 38
Titanic dataset 42
train_test_split function 11

W

Windows
  Scikit-learn, installing on 8

Thank you for buying
Learning scikit-learn: Machine Learning in Python

About Packt Publishing

Packt, pronounced 'packed', published its first book "*Mastering phpMyAdmin for Effective MySQL Management*" in April 2004 and subsequently continued to specialize in publishing highly focused books on specific technologies and solutions.

Our books and publications share the experiences of your fellow IT professionals in adapting and customizing today's systems, applications, and frameworks. Our solution based books give you the knowledge and power to customize the software and technologies you're using to get the job done. Packt books are more specific and less general than the IT books you have seen in the past. Our unique business model allows us to bring you more focused information, giving you more of what you need to know, and less of what you don't.

Packt is a modern, yet unique publishing company, which focuses on producing quality, cutting-edge books for communities of developers, administrators, and newbies alike. For more information, please visit our website: www.packtpub.com.

About Packt Open Source

In 2010, Packt launched two new brands, Packt Open Source and Packt Enterprise, in order to continue its focus on specialization. This book is part of the Packt Open Source brand, home to books published on software built around Open Source licences, and offering information to anybody from advanced developers to budding web designers. The Open Source brand also runs Packt's Open Source Royalty Scheme, by which Packt gives a royalty to each Open Source project about whose software a book is sold.

Writing for Packt

We welcome all inquiries from people who are interested in authoring. Book proposals should be sent to author@packtpub.com. If your book idea is still at an early stage and you would like to discuss it first before writing a formal book proposal, contact us; one of our commissioning editors will get in touch with you.

We're not just looking for published authors; if you have strong technical skills but no writing experience, our experienced editors can help you develop a writing career, or simply get some additional reward for your expertise.

open source
community experience distilled

Building Machine Learning Systems with Python

ISBN: 978-1-78216-140-0   Paperback: 290 pages

Master the art of machine learning with Python and build effective machine learning systems with this intensive hands-on guide

1. Master Machine Learning using a broad set of Python libraries and start building your own Python-based ML systems

2. Covers classification, regression, feature engineering, and much more guided by practical examples

Learning SciPy for Numerical and Scientific Computing

ISBN: 978-1-78216-162-2   Paperback: 150 pages

A practical tutorial that guarantees fast, accurate, and easy-to-code solutions to your numerical and scientific computing problems with the power of SciPy and Python

1. Perform complex operations with large matrices, including eigenvalue problems, matrix decompositions, or solution to large systems of equations

2. Step-by-step examples to easily implement statistical analysis and data mining that rivals in performance any of the costly specialized software suites

3. Plenty of examples of state-of-the-art research problems from all disciplines of science, that prove how simple, yet effective, is to provide solutions based on SciPy

Please check **www.PacktPub.com** for information on our titles

Python 3 Object Oriented Programming

ISBN: 978-1-84951-126-1   Paperback: 404 pages

Harness the power of Python 3 objects

1. Learn how to do Object Oriented Programming in Python using this step-by-step tutorial

2. Design public interfaces using abstraction, encapsulation, and information hiding

3. Turn your designs into working software by studying the Python syntax

4. Raise, handle, define, and manipulate exceptions using special error objects

Machine Learning with R

ISBN: 978-1-78216-214-8   Paperback: 396 pages

Learn how to use R to apply powerful machine learning methods and gain an insight into real-world applications

1. Harness the power of R for statistical computing and data science

2. Use R to apply common machine learning algorithms with real-world applications

3. Prepare, examine, and visualize data for analysis

4. Understand how to choose between machine learning models

Please check **www.PacktPub.com** for information on our titles

30762915R00068

Made in the USA
Lexington, KY
16 March 2014